3 All-Star

Workbook

Linda Lee ★ Stephen Sloan ★
Grace Tanaka ★ Shirley Velasco

Workbook by Kristin Sherman

McGraw-Hill

All-Star 3 Workbook

Published by McGraw-Hill ESL/ELT, a business unit of The McGraw-Hill Companies, Inc. 1221 Avenue of the Americas, New York, NY 10020. Copyright © 2005 by The McGraw-Hill Companies, Inc. All rights reserved. No part of this publication may be reproduced or distributed in any form or by any means, or stored in a database or retrieval system, without the prior written consent of The McGraw-Hill Companies, Inc., including, but not limited to, in any network or other electronic storage or transmission, or broadcast for distance learning.

ISBN 978-0-07-284680-5
MHID 0-07-284680-1
9 QPD/QPD 11 10 09

ISBN 978-0-07-111728-9 (International Workbook)
MHID 0-07-111728-8 (International Workbook)
2 3 4 5 6 7 8 9 QPD/QPD 11 10 09 08 07 06

Editorial director: Tina Carver
Executive editor: Erik Gundersen
Development editor: Linda O'Roke
Production manager: MaryRose Malley
Interior designer: Wee Design Group
Cover designer: Wee Design Group
Art: Andrew Lange, NETS/Carlos Sanchis

INTERNATIONAL EDITION ISBN 0-07-111728-8
Copyright © 2005. Exclusive rights by The McGraw-Hill Companies, Inc., for manufacture and export. This book cannot be re-exported from the country to which it is sold by McGraw-Hill. The International Edition is not available in North America.

McGraw-Hill

All-Star is a four-level, standards-based series for English learners featuring a picture-dictionary approach to vocabulary building. "Big picture" scenes in each unit provide springboards to a wealth of activities developing all of the language skills. Each *All Star* Workbook unit provides 14 pages of supplementary exercises for its corresponding Student Book unit. The Workbook activities offer students further practice in developing the language, vocabulary, and life-skill competencies taught in the Student Book. Answers to the Workbook activities are available in the Teacher's Edition.

Features

★ **Wide range of exercises** can be used by students working independently or in groups, in the classroom, with a tutor, or at home. Each lesson includes at least one activity which allows students to interact, usually by asking and answering questions.

★ **Alternate application lessons** complement the Student Book application lesson, inviting students to tackle work, family, and/or community extension activities in each unit. Each application lesson concludes with a *Take It Outside* activity, encouraging students to use the language skills they've learned in the unit to interact with others outside of the classroom. Some application lessons also have suggestions for a web-based activity. These *Take It Online* activities help students build computer skills while expanding on the content and the language skills they learned in the unit.

★ **Student Book page references** at the top of each Workbook page show how the two components support one another.

★ **Practice tests** at the end of each unit provide practice answering multiple-choice questions such as those found on the CASAS tests. Students are invited to chart their progress on these tests on a bar graph on the inside back cover.

★ **Spotlight: Grammar** lessons appear at the end of every other unit, offering supplementary grammar practice.

★ **Crossword puzzles and word searches** reinforce unit vocabulary.

Alternate Application Lessons (work, family, community)

Equipped for the Future (EFF) is a set of standards for adult literacy and lifelong learning, developed by The National Institute for Literacy (www.nifl.gov). The organizing principle of EFF is that adults assume responsibilities in three major areas of life—as workers, as parents, and as citizens. These three areas of focus are called "role maps" in the EFF documentation.

Lesson 6 in each unit of the Student Book provides a real-life application relating to one of the learners' roles. The Workbook includes two lessons, each of which addresses the other roles. This allows you, as the teacher, to customize the unit to meet the needs of your students. You can teach any or all of the application lessons in class. For example, if all your students work, you may choose to focus on the work applications. If your students have diverse interests and needs, you may have them work in small groups on different applications. If your program provides many hours of classroom time each week, you have enough material to cover all three roles.

Contents

Unit 6 Community

Unit 7 Work

Unit 8 Communication

LESSON 1

They have many responsibilities.

A Complete the paragraph below using the correct verb form (simple present, present continuous, or future). You may use verbs in the box more than once.

be	cook	do	go	have	meet	put
save	shop	study	take	wash	want	work

Laura and Ed Martin _____ always busy. Laura _____ full-time at a hotel, and Ed _____ an electrician. They _____ two children, Michael and Jennifer. They _____ to buy a new house, so they _____ money. The children _____ to school. Jennifer _____ her homework now. Laura _____ classes at the community college. She _____ hotel management. Both Laura and Ed _____ housework. Right now, Ed _____ away the groceries. He usually _____ and Laura usually _____ the meals. Michael often _____ the dishes. Next week, Laura and Ed _____ to a PTA meeting. They also _____ with someone at the bank about how to save money to buy a house.

B Look at the photo below. Complete the sentences.

1. The mother _____.

2. The father _____.

3. The daughter _____.

4. The family _____.

C Look at the pie graph. It shows how Laura spends her time on a typical day. Answer the questions.

1. How many hours does Laura study each day? _____

2. How many hours does she sleep? _____

3. How much time does Laura spend on housework? _____

4. How many hours does she work each day? _____

5. How many hours is Laura in class? _____

**Daily Activity Graph
(in 1 hour increments)**

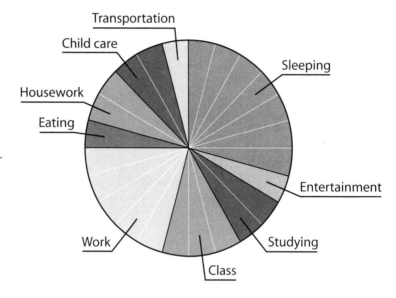

D Complete the table below. Write the amount of time you spend on each activity every day.

Activity	Time spent (in hours)
Sleeping	
Eating	
Studying	
Going to class	
Working	
Doing housework	
Taking care of children	
Commuting	
Reading, watching TV, seeing movies	
Other	

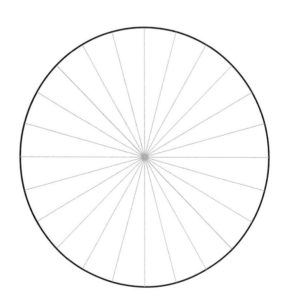

E Complete the pie graph above with the information from Activity D.

LESSON 2

I have to prioritize.

A Cross out the word that has a dissimilar meaning.

1. reduce   cut back   ~~add~~
2. pay off   increase debt   charge
3. tutor   teacher   student
4. focus   start   pay attention to
5. job bank   financial aid   loan
6. PTA   school meeting   practice
7. adult school   library   continuing education classes
8. interview   online job bank   newspaper job ads

B Read the paragraphs. Give two suggestions for each situation.

1. Boris wants to do take a course to become a certified nursing assistant. First, he must do well on an exam. Boris is not good at math, so he is worried about taking the math part of the exam. What do you think Boris should do?

Boris should get a tutor to help him with his math.

_____

_____

_____

2. Noriko would like to buy a car. She goes to school every day and works about 15 hours a week. Noriko doesn't like to cook, so she goes out to eat at least five times a week. What advice would you give Noriko?

_____

_____

_____

_____

3.   Mohamed wants to learn to use a computer. He would like to send emails to his family, but he is a little nervous about computers. What do you think Mohamed should do?

_____

_____

_____

_____

4.   Sara would like to change jobs. Right now, she is a salesclerk in a clothing store. She would like to become an accountant. Sara has children and is very busy. She doesn't think she has time to go back to school. What should Sara do?

_____

_____

_____

_____

C   Write the correct word form on the line.

Noun	Verb
application	apply
priority	_____
reduction	_____
_____	educate
_____	pay

5

What is a certificate program?

A Read the conversation.

Paul: Hi. I'm Paul Madison. I have an appointment with Tina Walker.

Tina: I'm Tina Walker. Please sit down. How can I help you today?

Paul: I'm planning on taking classes here at the community college in the fall, and I wanted to figure out which classes I should register for.

Tina: Okay. Have you finished high school?

Paul: No, but I got my GED.

Tina: Good. So you don't need adult high school or GED classes. Are you interested in a vocational certificate program, a two-year degree, or the college transfer program?

Paul: I'm not sure. What is a certificate program?

Tina: It's a short-term program in specific fields such as automotive technology, heating and air conditioning, and medical technology. You complete a certain number of courses and receive a certificate. A two-year degree program is longer, but when you finish, you have an Associate's degree. If you are interested in getting a four-year degree from a college or university, you probably want the college transfer program. What is your long-term goal?

Paul: I'd like to be an electrician.

Tina: Then you need the certificate program in electrical/electronics technology. Here is the college catalog. The description of your program is on page 39.

Paul: How long will it take me to finish?

Tina: If you take four courses each term, you should be finished in two terms.

B Answer the questions using complete sentences.

1. What do you think is Tina's job? _____

2. What kinds of programs are available at the community college? _____

   _____

   _____

3. What is Paul's long-term goal? _____

4. What program should Paul take to reach his goal? _____

C Read the information below.

CPCC Central Piedmont Community College

COLLEGE CATALOG | PROSPECTIVE STUDENTS | CURRENT STUDENTS | BUSINESS COMMUNITY

College Catalog and Programs of Study

Vocational Certificate (18 hours)	Associate in Applied Science (career-oriented program, 72 hours)	General Education (college transfer degree, at least 64 hours)
Automotive Maintenance Culinary Technology-Baking Electrical/Electronics Technology Heating and Air Conditioning Office Systems Technology Restaurant Management Welding	Accounting Computer Programming Culinary Arts Dental Hygiene Early Childhood Associate Electrical/Electronics Engineering Medical Assisting Physical Therapy Assisting	Associate in Arts (English, history, political science) Associate in Science (biology, psychology, engineering, architecture) Associate in Fine Arts (art, music, dance)

D Complete the chart.

Student	Area of study	Program of Study
Miriam wants to be the head chef in a restaurant.		
Jerome would like to study engineering at the university.		
Lana is interested in a two-year degree so she can be a physical therapy assistant.		
Rich wants to be a welder.		

TAKE IT OUTSIDE: Interview three family members, friends, or coworkers. Complete the chart.

Person interviewed	What they want to be doing five years from now	What they need to learn or do first to reach their goal

7

LESSON 4

A Success Story

A Read the introduction and fable by Aesop.

Aesop was a Greek writer in the 6th century B.C. He wrote stories called fables that were about animals. Aesop's fables ended with a lesson, or moral, that explained the meaning of the story.

A hare one day made fun of the short legs and slow pace of a tortoise, who replied, laughing: "Though you are fast as the wind, I can beat you in a race." The hare believed this was simply impossible and agreed to the race. On the day of the race the two started together. During the race, the tortoise never stopped for a moment. She went on with a slow but steady pace straight to the end of the course. The hare decided to rest by the side of the road and fell asleep. At last the hare woke up and ran as fast as he could. He saw the tortoise had reached the finish line and was comfortably resting after winning the race.

Moral: *Slow but steady wins the race.*

B Answer the questions.

1. What was the tortoise's goal? _____

2. How did she reach it? _____

3. Why did the hare lose the race? _____

4. Do you agree with the moral of the story? _____

C Read the proverbs. Write them in the correct box. Then add a proverb you know to each box.

1. Success has many friends.
2. Failures are but milestones on the road to success.
3. Success and rest don't sleep together.
4. Success has many parents, but failure is an orphan.
5. If you wish to succeed, consult three old people.

6. If at first you don't succeed, try, try again.

7. If you like to have things easy, you'll have difficulties; if you like problems, you will succeed.

8. Rome wasn't built in a day.

9. The early bird catches the worm.

You need to work hard to succeed.	
You will probably have some problems before you are successful.	
Other people can help you succeed.	*Success has many friends.*

D Answer the questions.

1. Which proverb from Activity C do you like best? Why?

_____

2. How are you successful? (What have you achieved?)

_____

3. What is one goal you achieved and how did you achieve it?

_____

_____

E Write a paragraph about a goal you achieved and how you achieved it on a separate piece of paper. Use your answers from Activity D.

LESSON

When she got home, she made dinner.

A Complete the sentences with the correct form of the verb in parentheses. More than one tense may be correct.

1. When Maggie comes, we _____ (leave).

2. When Val knocked on the door, I _____ (be) surprised.

3. You _____ (run) away when you saw me.

4. When they _____ (start) classes, they were nervous.

5. She _____ (write) when she has time.

6. We closed our books when the bell _____ (ring).

7. When my son comes home, I _____ (cook) dinner.

8. What _____ he _____ (do) when they close the store?

9. _____ you _____ (lock) the door when you left?

B Complete the questions. Use the future or past form of the verb.

1. A: _____ when you finish your homework? (what)
   B: I'm going to get some lunch.

2. A: _____ when he left school? (where)
   B: He went to work.

3. A: _____ when it snowed? (why)
   B: Classes were canceled because students couldn't get here.

4. A: _____ when you're in New York? (who)
   B: I'm going to visit my sister and my college roommate.

5. A: _____ when she gets home?
   B: I think so. I told her to call right away.

6. A: _____ when they went to the library?
   B: No, they didn't get books, they got a video.

10

C Answer the questions about you. Use complete sentences.

1. What did you do when you first arrived in this city?

_____

2. Where did you live when you were 15?

_____

3. How did you feel when you started this class?

_____

4. Who did you look up to when you were a child?

_____

5. What are you going to do when you leave class today?

_____

6. Where will you live when you are 80?

_____

7. Who are you going to visit when you go on your next trip?

_____

D Look at the pictures. Write sentences. Describe what you will do the next time you are in these situations.

_____

_____

_____

_____

_____

_____

_____

_____

FAMILY

LESSON

Talking To Your Child's Teacher

A Read the information.

How to Communicate Better with Your Child's School

One of the most important things you can do to help your child succeed in school is to attend a parent-teacher conference. Just like any important meeting, you can make it a positive experience by following certain steps.

Before the meeting:

1. Schedule an appointment if you need to talk to the teacher. Write a note or make a phone call to set up a convenient time.
2. Gather information. Talk to your child and your spouse and/or other caregivers. Ask what concerns or questions they have.
3. Make a list of what you want to talk about. This will help you remember everything and stay on topic.

During the meeting:

4. Build the relationship. Make small talk. Compliment the teacher if he or she is doing something well.
5. Ask questions about the class and how your child is doing.
6. Deal with problems in a positive way. Ask for specific examples of problems and what seems to help. Develop a plan with the teacher for dealing with the problem in the future. Schedule a time to follow up on the problem. Make sure you know what the teacher will do next.

After the meeting:

7. Talk to your child about the good things he or she is doing and how any problems will be addressed.
8. Follow up with the teacher.

Throughout the year:

9. Stay in touch with the teacher through notes or phone calls.
10. Volunteer at school in the classroom, lunchroom, or library.

B Complete the sentences using information from Activity A.

1. When you want to talk to the teacher, you should _____ an appointment for a convenient time.

2. If you talk to your child or spouse before the meeting, you can _____ information.

3. Before the meeting, you should make a _____ of what you want to talk about.

4. _____ the meeting you should ask questions about the class.

5. You can build a relationship with the teacher by making _____ _____.

C Read the sentences. What are they examples of? Write the number of the step from Activity A.

1. "Your teacher said you got an award in math." _____
2. "I'd like to talk to you about Katie's grades. When would be a good time to get together?" _____
3. "Katie is really enjoying your class. She is very excited about school this year." _____
4. "How is Katie's reading?" _____
5. "So in the next week, you will work with Katie on taking notes, and we will monitor how she focuses on homework. Then we'll talk next week." _____
6. "Do you need any help? I'm available on Mondays." _____

D Unscramble the words to form questions.

1. school/your child/like/does

   _____?

2. what/does/your child/well/do

   _____?

3. your child/what/in school/problems/have/does

   _____?

★ ★

TAKE IT OUTSIDE: Ask a family member, friend, or coworker the questions in Activity D. Write their answers.

1. _____
2. _____
3. _____

★ ★

TAKE IT ONLINE: Use your favorite search engine to find out about "parent-teacher communication." Write down three ideas.

_____

_____

_____

13

COMMUNITY
LESSON

Becoming a Citizen

A Answer the questions about yourself.

1. When did you move to this country? _____

2. How long will you live here? _____

3. Do you like the United States? _____

4. Would you like to become a citizen? _____

5. Why or why not? _____

6. What country are you a citizen of now? _____

B Read the information about becoming a U.S. citizen.

⊠ ⊟ ⊞   **USCIS.GOV**

U.S. Citizenship and Immigration Services

HOME   WHAT'S NEW   FAQS   SEARCH   GLOSSARY   FEEDBACK   TRANSLATE   PRINT

About Us and FOIA

Citizenship

Immigration Forms, Fees and Fingerprints

Immigration Services and Benefits Programs

Services Field Office Addresses and Information

Immigration Laws, Regulations, and Guides

USCIS Public Affairs

Working for Immigration Programs

Other Government Sites

USCIS.gov

Welcome to the naturalization home page. Naturalization is the process by which U.S. citizenship is conferred upon a foreign citizen or national after he or she fulfills the requirements established by Congress in the Immigration and Nationality Act (INA). The general requirements for administrative naturalization include:

• a period of continuous residence and physical presence in the United States;

• residence in a particular USCIS District prior to filing;

• an ability to read, write, and speak English;

• a knowledge and understanding of U.S. history and government;

• good moral character;

• attachment to the principles of the U.S. Constitution; and,

• favorable disposition toward the United States.

14

C | Match the phrase to its meaning.

1. ____ a period of continuous residence and physical presence in the United States

2. ____ a knowledge and understanding of U.S. history and government

3. ____ good moral character

4. ____ attachment to the principles of the U.S. Constitution

5. ____ favorable disposition toward the United States

a. liking the United States

b. knowing about U.S. history and government

c. being a good person

d. living in the United States for a certain period of time

e. believing in U.S. laws

D | Check *True* or *False*. Use the information from Activity B.

If you want become a citizen,

1. you have to know about U.S. history. ☐ True ☐ False

2. you can live in another country some of the time. ☐ True ☐ False

3. you need to have a certain amount of money. ☐ True ☐ False

4. you have to follow U.S. laws. ☐ True ☐ False

5. you need to marry an American. ☐ True ☐ False

6. you should like the U.S. ☐ True ☐ False

★ ★

TAKE IT OUTSIDE: Interview a family member, friend, or coworker who is a citizen of the U.S. Ask the questions. Write their answers.

1. Were you born in the U.S.? _____

2. If not, when did you move here? _____

3. When did you become a citizen? _____

4. What is a responsibility you have as a citizen? _____

   _____

5. What do you think are the qualities of a good citizen? _____

   _____

★ ★

TAKE IT ONLINE: Use your favorite search engine to find out about the naturalization process. Find the answers to the questions below.

1. How many years do you have to live here before you can apply? _____

2. How many years do you have to wait to apply if you are married to an American citizen? _____

3. What is the first step in the application process? _____

REVIEW

LESSON

Practice Test

DIRECTIONS: Look at the pie chart below to answer the next five questions. Use the Answer Sheet.

Student Goals

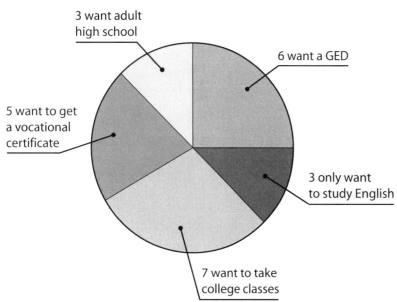

3 want adult high school

6 want a GED

5 want to get a vocational certificate

3 only want to study English

7 want to take college classes

ANSWER SHEET

1 Ⓐ Ⓑ Ⓒ Ⓓ
2 Ⓐ Ⓑ Ⓒ Ⓓ
3 Ⓐ Ⓑ Ⓒ Ⓓ
4 Ⓐ Ⓑ Ⓒ Ⓓ
5 Ⓐ Ⓑ Ⓒ Ⓓ
6 Ⓐ Ⓑ Ⓒ Ⓓ
7 Ⓐ Ⓑ Ⓒ Ⓓ
8 Ⓐ Ⓑ Ⓒ Ⓓ
9 Ⓐ Ⓑ Ⓒ Ⓓ
10 Ⓐ Ⓑ Ⓒ Ⓓ

1. What does the pie chart show?

   A. how much time students spend on their goals

   B. students' educational goals

   C. students' occupations

   D. students' ages

2. How many students want to get a vocational certificate?

   A. 3   C. 6

   B. 5   D. 7

3. How many students want to get a GED?

   A. 3   C. 6

   B. 5   D. 7

4. Which is the goal of the most students?

   A. to get a GED

   B. to take adult high school classes

   C. to take college classes

   D. to get a vocational certificate

5. Which goal of those below do the smallest number of students want to achieve?

   A. to get a GED

   B. to take adult high school classes

   C. to take college classes

   D. to get a vocational certificate

DIRECTIONS: Read the article to answer the next five questions. Use the Answer Sheet on page 16.

How to Succeed in School

You can do well in school if you follow certain steps. First, you should think about how you learn best. Do you like to see and read information? Then you may be a visual learner. Do you like to hear people tell you information? You may be an auditory learner. Do you learn best if you actually do something? Then you might be a hands-on learner. The following ideas can help different learners do well.

1. Take good notes to read later.
2. Ask questions.
3. Make a model.
4. Review information within 24 hours to remember it.
5. Don't give up.

---

6. Which strategy will help students who like to read information?

   A. 1
   B. 2
   C. 3
   D. 4

7. Which strategy will help students remember new vocabulary words?

   A. 1
   B. 4
   C. 5
   D. All the above

8. What should students do if they don't understand what the teacher says?

   A. take good notes
   B. ask questions
   C. practice
   D. review information within 24 hours

9. If students want to succeed, what should they do first?

   A. figure out how they learn best
   B. give up
   C. study every 24 hours
   D. follow the teacher

10. If you like to learn things by doing, what will help you?

    A. talking to the teacher
    B. making a model
    C. listening to tapes
    D. watching a video

HOW DID YOU DO? Count the number of correct answers on your answer sheet. Record this number in the bar graph on the inside back cover.

Spotlight: Reading

A Read the following article. Underline the important words or phrases that help you guess the meaning of the words in bold.

Keep Your Brain Young

Medical researchers suggest that we can keep our brains young as we grow old. Usually people experience memory loss and a decrease in **cognitive** ability as their brains get older. Research shows that we can slow this process down by keeping our brains **active**. In other words, we need to "use it or lose it."

Doing crossword puzzles, playing word games, and other **mental** exercises gives our brains the work they need to stay healthy. Taking classes can train our brains to do new things. When our brains focus and solve problems, they are getting exercise.

People can improve their memory through physical exercise as well. **Recall** ability increased after six months of regular aerobic exercise, such as running or swimming.

A good diet can also help with cognitive **function**. People who ate green leafy vegetables stayed sharper mentally than people who did not.

Adapted from "Train your brain to go the distance", *Charlotte Observer* 8/25/04

B Choose the word with the closest meaning to the words in **bold**. Circle the correct answer.

1. Usually people experience memory loss and a decrease in **cognitive** ability as their brains get older.

   A. physical　　　　B. thinking　　　　C. musical

2. Research shows that we can slow this process down by keeping our brains **active**.

   A. busy　　　　B. quiet　　　　C. slow

3. Taking a class, learning a new language, and other **mental** exercises give our brains the work they need to stay healthy.

   A. writing　　　　B. physical　　　　C. thinking

4. People can improve their memory through physical exercise as well. **Recall** ability increased after six months of regular aerobic exercise, such as running or swimming.

   A. memory   B. running   c. healthy

5. A good diet can also help with cognitive **function**.

   A. food   B. exercise   c. activity

C   Write definitions for the words in **bold**.

1. Many older people have **diminished** brain function, and so have memory loss and other problems in thinking.

   _____

2. When you **concentrate** on solving a problem, you focus your attention on it. This exercises your brain.

   _____

3. Physical **fitness** improves your body's health, of course, but it also aids your mental health.

   _____

4. You increase your **intellectual** activity if you take a class, learn a new skill, or play a difficult game.

   _____

5. People don't have to have a **decline** in their quality of life as they age—they can prevent many of the negative effects of aging by exercising, eating well, and working with their brains.

   _____

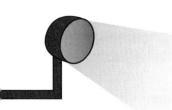

Spotlight: Writing

A Look at the cluster diagram below. Write the ideas in the correct place on the chart.

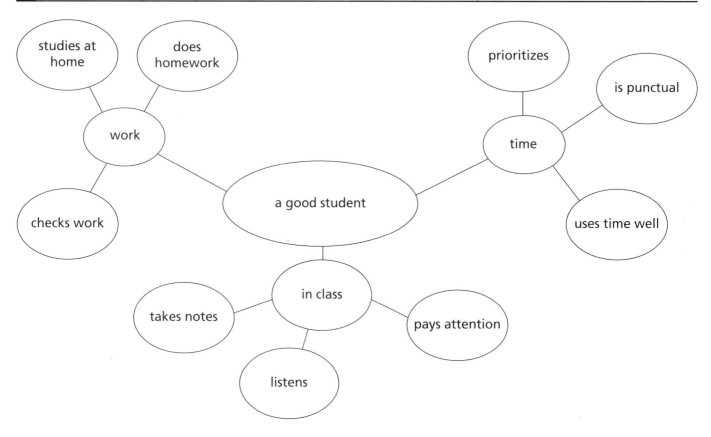

A GOOD STUDENT		
work	**time**	**in class**
studies at home		

B Write three sentences about the qualities of a good student. Use the information in Activity A.

EXAMPLE: *A good student studies at home.*

1. _____

2. _____

3. _____

C   Answer the questions.

1. Who was your favorite teacher?

   _____

2. Why did you like him or her?

   _____

3. What kinds of things do you think a good teacher does in class?

   _____

4. How is a good teacher like a good student?

   _____

D   Create a cluster diagram in the space below to describe the qualities of a good teacher.

a good teacher

E   Write three sentences about the qualities of a good teacher.

1. _____

2. _____

3. _____

LESSON 1

What are the pluses and minuses?

A Look at the photos. Write sentences about the houses, using the cues below.

Jill's house

Rob's house

1. (chimney) *Rob's house has a chimney, but Jill's doesn't.* _____

2. (driveway) _____

3. (lots of windows) _____

4. (garage) _____

5. (fenced yard) _____

6. (porch) _____

7. (lots of trees) _____

B Complete the sentences.

1. I'd like to keep my car inside, so a _____ is important to me.

2. We have two dogs. We would like a _____ .

3. If the house has a fireplace, it must have a _____ .

4. It's hot here in the summer. I'd like a house with _____ for shade.

5. My parents like being outside, but they want to sit at a table. They'd like a house with a _____ .

6. When it snows we have to shovel the _____ before we can take the car out.

7. Right now our apartment is very dark. When we move, we want a house with _____ .

22

C Answer the questions about the houses in Activity A.

1. Whose house do you think is more expensive? Why? _____

_____

2. Which house do you prefer? Why? _____

_____

3. In what part of the country do you think you would find each of the houses? Why? _____

_____

D Read the paragraph below. Whose house from Activity A does it describe?

This beautiful home is in a quiet residential neighborhood. The yard is a good size and has many trees. The very comfortable living room has a fireplace, and there is a garage attached to the house. The upstairs bedrooms have a wonderful attic charm. The sidewalks add to the neighborhood's safety.

House: _____

E Write a paragraph and describe the other house from Activity A.

_____

_____

_____

_____

_____

F Combine two words below to form compound nouns. Refer to Activities A and D.

back ✓	case	side
bath	drive	stair
bed	fire	walk
book	place	way
	room	yard ✓

backyard _____   _____

_____   _____

_____   _____

_____   _____

23

It's available immediately.

A Look at the ads. Write the word next to each abbreviation.

SALE

A Home in university area! 3BR/2BA, 2-car gar., wash/dry, elec, AC., fncd yd., $179,000. 617-555-5612

D CONDO—2BR, 1.5 BA, garden unit, w/d, pool, prvt. Patio, $69,000. Call 508-555-0998

RENT

B HOUSE – 4 BR/2.5 BA, 2-car gar., fp, fncd, WD hookups. Pets ok. $825/mo. Available immed. 414-555-7612

E TOWNHOME—2 BR, gar., bk yrd, deck W/d conn., appls. Avail. Immed. 617-555-1333

RENT

C APT FURN – Nice 1BR , 1 person, all util., sec. dep. Ref. $125 week. No pets. 414-555-1630

F APARTMENT – Cascade Circle, 2BR big yard, quiet nghbrhd, pch, appls., Pets ok. $600/mo. 508-555-4962

BR _____   util. _____

BA _____   dep. _____

AC _____   avail. _____

elec. _____   prkg. _____

B Read the following situations. Which place from Activity A would be best for each situation? Write the letter of the ad.

"I just moved to town and need a place to live. I'd like to rent a small apartment for a few weeks until I know what part of town I want to live in. I can't pay more than $550 a month."

"My husband and I have a wonderful daughter, and are expecting twins in six months. We also have a dog. We want to buy a house."

Which ad do you think Tan would like? _____   Which ad would Linda be interested in? _____

"My husband died last year, so Buster and I live alone now. He's a great companion. I don't need my big house anymore. I'd like to live in a two-bedroom apartment with a yard for Buster."

"We moved here two months ago and are staying with my brother Hugo. My wife Nadia wants to move to a house. We can't afford to buy yet. We want at least three bedrooms."

Which ad would Doris like best? _____   Which ad do you think Martin would like? _____

C Look at the ads in Activity A. Answer the questions.

1. How much is the two-bedroom apartment a month?   _____

2. Are utilities included in the rent for the one-bedroom apartment?   _____

3. Does the condo have a pool?   _____

4. How much is the three-bedroom house?   _____

D Practice the strategy of grouping words. Complete the chart below with words to describe your home.

Words that describe your home	Parts of your home
small	dining room

E Write an ad for your home. Use words from Activity D and abbreviations when appropriate.

_____

_____

_____

_____

My air conditioner isn't working.

3 LESSON

A Put the conversation in order from 1 to 9.

_____ Okay. I'll check it out as soon as I can.

_____ Maybe 2:30.

___1___ Hello. This is Ed.

_____ You're welcome. Good-bye.

_____ Yes. What can I do for you?

_____ Well. My air conditioner isn't working.

_____ Can you give me a more exact time?

_____ Hi. This is Sandra Peterson in Apartment 103B.

_____ That's great. Thanks. I'll see you then.

B Answer the questions.

1. Who is the tenant? _____

2. Where does she live? _____

3. Who is the landlord? _____

4. What is the problem? _____

5. What time will Ed come? _____

C Complete the form for the problem in Activity A. Use today's date.

> **Southside Property Management**
> Maintenance Request Form
>
> Tenant's name: _____   Date: _____
>
> Apt. # _____
>
> Description of problem: _____
>
> _____
>
> Date and approximate time of maintenance visit: _____

D Look at the photos. Describe the problem to your landlord or building manager.

This is your tenant in Apartment 7G. I'm calling to report

a problem with _____

_____

_____

_____

_____

_____

_____

_____

★ ★

TAKE IT OUTSIDE: Interview a family member, friend, or co-worker. Ask the three questions below. Then write a paragraph about the problem.

1. What is one problem you had with your house or apartment last year?

2. Did you get help with the problem?

3. How was the problem solved?

_____

_____

_____

★ ★

Renter's Insurance

LESSON 4

A Read the article from a website.

⊠ ⊟ ⊞   RENTER'S INSURANCE

DEPARTMENT OF INSURANCE

Consumer Advice

Publications

Services

Consumer Issues

Company Lists

Complaint Info

File a Complaint

Look Up Company

Site Map

Look Up Agent

FAQ Search

Renter's Insurance

(Revised May 2004)

News reports of apartment fires often include **tragic** stories of renters who've lost everything because they weren't insured. A landlord's insurance usually covers the building, but not the personal property of residents. If you rent an apartment, duplex, house, or townhouse, you may need renter's insurance to protect your **belongings**.

How Renter's Insurance Works

Renter's insurance is a type of residential property coverage specifically designed for people who rent houses or apartments. These policies are often called "tenant policies."

Renter's insurance

- pays to repair or replace personal property that's damaged, destroyed, or stolen. Limits on this coverage vary by policy, but most provide at least $4,000 worth of protection. Policies may limit payments for certain kinds of property, however. Common **maximums** are $100 for lost cash; $2,500 for personal property used for business; $500 for valuable papers; and $500 for theft of jewelry, watches, and furs. Renter's insurance also covers your luggage and other personal items when you travel for up to 10 percent of the amount of your policy or $1,000, whichever is greater.

- pays living expenses, such as motel costs, if you're **displaced** from your home or apartment. This "loss of use" coverage is generally limited to 20 percent of a policy's personal property coverage. For example, if you have $25,000 in personal property coverage, your loss-of-use coverage would be $5,000. You would be paid up to this amount for the reasonable time required to repair or replace your rented property.

- provides **liability** coverage if you are legally responsible for another person's injury or property damage. If someone is injured in your home and **files a lawsuit**, a renter's policy automatically provides $25,000 in liability coverage and pays your legal costs. Extra liability coverage is available for an additional premium.

B Circle the correct answers.

1. What does renter's insurance cover?

   A. the tenant's things   B. the apartment   C. a car   D. medical problems

2. What are common amounts that renter's insurance would pay for property used for business?

   A. $100   B. $500   C. $2,500   D. $1000

28

3. When will renter's insurance help pay for motel costs?

   A. if you are injured   B. if you get a lawyer   C. if you have to leave because of damage   D. if you paid the premium

4. What does liability coverage pay for?

   A. someone injured in your home   B. loss of use   C. jewelry and furs   D. luggage on a trip

5. According to the information on the website, which amount of coverage is the largest?

   A. luggage   B. personal property   C. loss of use   D. lost cash

C Match the words from Activity A with the correct definitions. Use the context to guess the meanings.

Word	Definition
1. _____ tragic	a. the largest possible amount
2. _____ belongings	b. to take someone to court
3. _____ maximum	c. legal responsibility to pay
4. _____ displaced	d. things that you own
5. _____ liability	e. very sad
6. _____ file a lawsuit	f. forced to leave

D List the approximate amount it would take to replace your property in the chart below. Write NA (*not applicable*) next to items you don't own.

Property	Replacement value
Furniture	
TV, VCR, Stereo, Tapes, CDs, DVDs	
Computer	
Microwave oven	
Other appliances	
Clothing	
Kitchenware	
Sports equipment	
Cameras	
Books	
Jewelry	
All other property	
TOTAL PERSONAL PROPERTY	

E Complete the word forms chart below with words from the reading.

Nouns	Verbs	Adjectives
_____	replace	replaceable
person	personalize	_____
_____	XXXXXX	liable
resident	reside	_____
reason	reason	_____

LESSON 5

Which do you think is the best?

A Read the chart below. Write sentences with comparatives, superlatives, or expressions with *as/not as*. Use the cues in parentheses.

Dishwasher Ratings

Excellent ✓✓✓   Good ✓✓   Fair ✓

Dishwasher Brand	Price	How Large	How Clean	How Quiet	How Easy To Use
Baker	$520	✓✓	✓✓✓	✓	✓✓
Content	$870	✓	✓✓	✓✓	✓✓✓
Washmaster	$1200	✓✓✓	✓✓✓	✓✓✓	✓

1. The Baker dishwasher is _____ (cheap).

2. The Washmaster dishwasher is _____ (expensive).

3. The Content dishwasher is _____ (easy) to use.

4. The Baker gets the dishes _____ (clean) the Washmaster.

5. The Washmaster gets the dishes _____ (clean) the Content Dishwasher.

6. The Baker dishwasher is _____ (noisy) the other two.

7. The Washmaster is _____ (quiet).

8. The Washmaster is _____ (easy) to use as the Baker dishwasher.

9. The Content is _____ (small). The Washmaster is _____ (big).

10. The Baker is _____ (large) as the Washmaster.

B Which dishwasher do you think is the best? Why? _____

_____

_____

C Answer the questions. Write complete sentences using comparatives, superlatives, or expressions with *as/not as*.

EXAMPLE: *I'd rather take classes in the evening because the time is more convenient.*

1. When would you rather take classes—in the evening or in the morning? Why?

   _____

2. What is your favorite kind of food and why?

   _____

3. Would you rather live in an apartment or a house? Why?

   _____

4. What is the worst housing problem you have had?

   _____

5. Where is the best place to live and why?

   _____

D Look at the photo. Write a paragraph and compare this house to your home. Use comparatives and expressions with *as/not as*.

_____

_____

_____

_____

_____

How safe is your home?

A Look at the title of the article and the photos in Activity B. What do you think the article is about? Check the main idea.

❑ Children's furniture ❑ Keeping your children safe at home ❑ How to play with your baby

B Read the article. Check the childproofing tips that you follow now.

CHILDPROOF YOUR HOME

If you are expecting a baby or have small children in your home, you should childproof your home immediately. Look at your house from a toddler's point of view. Get down on the floor and look for dangers: places where a child could get a shock, a burn, or a cut.

Safety in the bathroom:

❑ Keep medications and cleaners out of the reach of children.

❑ Put non-slip mats in the shower and tub.

❑ Check the water temperature before you put your child in it.

❑ Supervise children under six years of age when they are in the bathtub.

❑ Keep electrical appliances away from the water.

Safety in the kitchen:

❑ Put childproof latches on cabinets.

❑ Keep electrical appliances and cords out of the reach of children.

❑ Turn pot handles away.

❑ Cook on back burners.

❑ Keep sharp knives in a locked drawer or out of reach.

❑ Supervise young children using the microwave.

❑ Don't carry hot liquids and a child.

Safety in the bedroom and living room:

❑ Cover electrical outlets with plastic covers.

❑ Wrap cords for curtains and blinds up out of reach.

❑ Keep small items out of reach so children won't swallow them.

❑ Put locks on windows.

❑ Use a child safety gate at the top and bottom of the stairs.

❑ Keep plants out of reach. Some are poisonous.

❑ Put padding on sharp edges such as the fireplace.

C Check *True* or *False*.

	True	False
1. You can see all the dangers in your house if you walk around.	☐	☐
2. You should put latches on cabinets so children can't open them.	☐	☐
3. You shouldn't cook on the back burners.	☐	☐
4. It's okay to leave small objects around the house.	☐	☐
5. The cords for blinds and curtains can be dangerous.	☐	☐
6. Microwaves are safe for children to use.	☐	☐

D Answer the questions using information from Activity B.

1. What are three things you can do so children don't get burns?

_____

2. What are two ways to prevent falls?

_____

3. How can you make sure children don't get a shock?

_____

E List three things you think new parents should buy to make their homes safer.

1. _____
2. _____
3. _____

★ ★

TAKE IT OUTSIDE: Interview a friend, family member or coworker. Write their answers in the chart.

Children's names and ages	Dangers in their home?	How their home is childproofed

★ ★

TAKE IT ONLINE: Use your favorite search engine to find information on childproofing your home. List three new ideas for making your home safer.

_____

_____

_____

33

Allocating Resources

A Look at a company's floor plan below. Circle the correct answer.

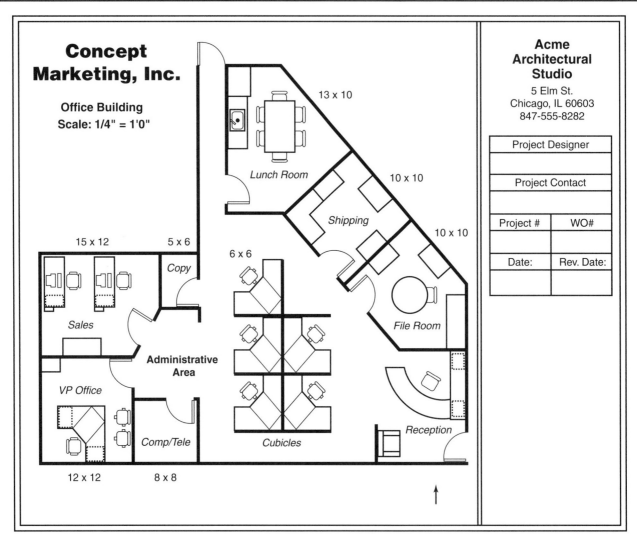

1. Where is the VP's (vice president's) office?

   A. next to the sales office

   B. across from the file room

   C. next to the shipping room

   D. behind reception

2. Where is the lunch room?

   A. across from the copy room

   B. next to the VP's office

   C. next to shipping

   D. across from reception

3. Which room is the largest?

   A. the lunch room

   B. the VP's office

   C. the shipping room

   D. the sales area

B Find the area of the rooms in Concept Marketing offices. Multiply the length by the width to get the square footage. Write the numbers.

EXAMPLE: Copy room *5* x *6* = *30* square feet

1. Vice president's office _____ x _____ = _____ square feet

2. Cubicle _____ x _____ = _____ square feet

3. Sales area _____ x _____ = _____ square feet

4. Computer/Telephone area _____ x _____ = _____ square feet

5. Shipping _____ x _____ = _____ square feet

C Read the situations. Answer the questions.

1. You need to put carpeting down in all five cubicles of Concepts Marketing. How many square feet of carpet do you need? _____

2. You need to put down wood flooring in the vice-president's office, the sales area, the copy room, the computer/telephone area, and the administrative area. How many square feet of flooring will you need? _____

3. Concept Marketing needs a telephone in every room and one on every desk. How many telephone lines will they need? _____

D Someone is coming today to install new computers in the sales area. Write directions to tell him how to reach the sales area from the front door.

_____

_____

★ ★
TAKE IT OUTSIDE: Measure the rooms in your home or office. Write the total square feet here: _____.
★ ★

Practice Test

DIRECTIONS: Read the housing ads to answer the next five questions. Use the Answer Sheet.

For Rent	For Rent
Area 1	Area 2
APARTMENT. Lrg. 3 BR, nr trans., small pets OK. Utils. Incl. $900/month. Call 555-8990.	SOUTH END. 4 BR house. Lrg. fncd yd. Pets OK. Modern & bright. New kitchen. $1000 + util, sec. Dep. 555-2340.
CONDO. 2 BR, 1 BA. Prkg, patio. Newly remod., new carpet. No pets, No smoke. $875. 555-6777.	HOUSE. 3 BR, 2.5 BA. Pool, nice yd., 2-car garage. Nr school & shopping. $1100. 555-9042.

ANSWER SHEET

1	Ⓐ	Ⓑ	Ⓒ	Ⓓ
2	Ⓐ	Ⓑ	Ⓒ	Ⓓ
3	Ⓐ	Ⓑ	Ⓒ	Ⓓ
4	Ⓐ	Ⓑ	Ⓒ	Ⓓ
5	Ⓐ	Ⓑ	Ⓒ	Ⓓ
6	Ⓐ	Ⓑ	Ⓒ	Ⓓ
7	Ⓐ	Ⓑ	Ⓒ	Ⓓ
8	Ⓐ	Ⓑ	Ⓒ	Ⓓ
9	Ⓐ	Ⓑ	Ⓒ	Ⓓ
10	Ⓐ	Ⓑ	Ⓒ	Ⓓ

1. You are looking for a house to rent. Which area should you look in?

A. Area 1

B. Area 2

C. Area 3

D. Area 4

2. You want an apartment near a bus line or subway stop. Which number should you call?

A. 555-8990

B. 555-6777

C. 555-2340

D. 555-9042

3. You only want two bedrooms. How much is the rent?

A. $900

B. $875

C. $1000

D. $1100

4. You want a garage. Which ad meets your needs?

A. apartment

B. condo

C. 4-bedroom house

D. 3-bedroom house

5. You have a cat. Which ad is not appropriate for you?

A. apartment

B. condo

C. 4-bedroom house

D. 3-bedroom house

DIRECTIONS: Read the information about tenant's rights to answer the next five questions. Use the Answer Sheet on page 36.

> Landlords should maintain the property in a clean and safe condition. Leases usually state that the tenant has a responsibility to notify the landlord of any repairs needed. Even if there is no lease, a tenant should give the landlord notice of a problem because some defects can cause serious damage. For example, a water leak may damage ceilings, floors, carpet, and appliances. When you tell the landlord right away, the landlord is less likely to charge you for the repairs or deduct money from your security deposit. If you, as the tenant, are responsible for the damage, either because you caused it or you failed to report a problem, you may have to pay for the repairs. If it's an emergency such as a broken pipe, you should tell or call your landlord immediately. When you notify the landlord of a problem in writing, keep a copy for your records.

6. Why should you report problems immediately?

   A. A small problem can cause a lot of damage.

   B. The landlord may get mad at you.

   C. The lease says you have to.

   D. You don't get a security deposit.

7. When might you have to pay for a repair?

   A. The landlord doesn't make a repair.

   B. You don't have a lease.

   C. You caused the problem.

   D. It's a water leak.

8. What is a benefit of reporting a problem right away?

   A. The landlord is less likely to charge you for it.

   B. You will get a new lease.

   C. You get a copy of the notice.

   D. You get a new apartment.

9. In which situation, would the landlord probably pay for the repair?

   A. Someone spilled tomato sauce on the carpet.

   B. Your son broke a window.

   C. There is a leak in the roof that is 8 months old, but you didn't report it.

   D. A pipe broke in the bathroom.

10. What are ways to notify the landlord of a problem?

   A. by phone

   B. in person

   C. in writing

   D. all the above

HOW DID YOU DO? Count the number of correct answers on your answer sheet. Record this number in the bar graph on the inside back cover.

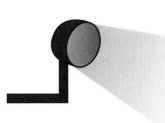

Spotlight: Reading

A Look at the subtitles of the article in Activity E. Write three questions based on the subtitles. Then predict answers to the questions.

Questions   **Possible answers**

1. _____   _____

2. _____   _____

3. _____   _____

B Look at the photos for the article in Activity E. Write a sentence about each.

_____

_____

C Read the first sentence in each paragraph of the article in Activity E. Check the predictions you agree with.

I think this information is about

- ☐ how to keep your home safe.
- ☐ low cost housing.
- ☐ public places to visit.
- ☐ how the government helps keep rents low.
- ☐ how to fill out rental applications.
- ☐ different types of housing.
- ☐ where to find the best apartments.

D List three things you already know about this topic.

1. _____

2. _____

3. _____

E Read the article. Check your answers.

Low-Income Housing

There are several low-income housing options that allow families and individuals to live in safe and affordable homes. These options include public housing, Section 8 housing vouchers, and privately owned apartments and houses that receive subsidies from the government to provide low cost homes.

Public Housing

Through the Department of Housing and Urban Development (HUD), the U.S. government provides money to counties and cities to build Public Housing Facilities. The counties and cities manage these housing developments. The rent is based on the family's income and size. Rent cannot be more than 30 percent of the family's total income. Only families who are low income can live in public housing. There are about 1.3 million families currently living in public housing.

To apply, you should contact your local housing authority or the HUD field office. You will need to list all the people who would live in the home, your current address and phone number, names and addresses of previous landlords, your income and employment information.

Section 8 Vouchers

The federal government also offers another program for low-income families: Section 8 vouchers. People who live in an area where housing is expensive often spend too much on housing. If you meet the income requirements, you can apply for vouchers that will pay the difference between the 30% you should pay on rent and the appropriate market rent. The money is paid directly to the landlord by the Public Housing Authority. There is often a long waiting list for Section 8 vouchers, and a family's place on the list depends on its income, size, and citizenship status.

Privately owned subsidized housing

The government gives money directly to the owner so that rents can be low. The landlord applies that money to the rents he/she charges low-income tenants. Privately owned apartments, town homes, and houses are available for seniors, people with disabilities, and families and individuals who qualify for low cost housing. You can get a list of subsidized properties through the HUD website.

Spotlight: Writing

A We write both personal and business letters. Read the personal letter below and answer the questions.

> Dear Greta,
>
> I'm writing this letter to let you know some good news. I'm moving to New York next month. I got a new job, and it's located in Albany. I'm going to start work in about six weeks. I'm pretty excited. It will be great to see you more. I miss my favorite cousin!
>
> My new address will be 6583 Meadow St., Albany, NY, 12202. You can always reach me at my email address: luketheduke@vbath.net.
>
> > Take care,
> > Luke

1. What is the purpose of the letter? _____

2. What is the relationship between the writer and the reader? _____

3. What is going to happen? _____

4. When will it happen? _____

5. Where is Luke going? _____

6. How can Greta contact Luke? _____

B Write a personal letter to a friend.

_____,

_____

_____

_____

_____

_____

               _____,

               _____

C Read the business letter below. Answer the questions.

Dear Customer:

This letter is to inform you of the area code change that will take place in Hopkins County. Your new area code will be 945. This change becomes effective on August 17, 2005 after which time callers will need to use the 945 area code to complete calls to this area.

You may contact Midsouth Telcom by calling 800-555-9000. Additional information can be found on the Midsouth Telcom website at http://www.mdstel.com.

Sincerely,
Your Midsouth Telcom team

---

1. What is the purpose of this letter? _____

2. What is the relationship between the writer and the reader? _____

3. Why is Midsouth sending the letter? _____

4. What is going to happen? _____

5. When will it happen? _____

6. Who will be affected? _____

7. How or where can people get more information? _____

D Write a letter to a landlord. Include the information below.

To: Robert Coles   **Why:** You, the writer, will move and will not renew your lease
When: next month   **Where:** Apartment 10A, Greenbriar Apartments
Contact: 555-8722

Dear _____ :

_____

_____

_____

_____

_____ ,

_____

LESSON 1

Are you healthy?

A Take the survey. Check the things you do now.

How healthy are you?

_____ drink 6–8 glasses of water every day

_____ exercise at least 20 minutes, 5 days a week

_____ eat 4–6 servings of vegetables a day

_____ eat red meat only once or twice a week

_____ don't smoke

_____ wear sunblock or stay out of the sun

_____ don't drink soda

_____ limit my intake of salt and sugar

_____ sleep at least 7 hours a night

_____ always wear a seatbelt in the car

_____ check my blood pressure regularly

B Cross out the word or phrase that has a dissimilar meaning.

1. ~~healthy~~	unhealthy	bad for your health
2. nutritious food	healthy food	junk food
3. well-protected	safe	unprotected
4. sunny	clear	cloudy
5. shade	sun	sunblock
6. relaxed	nervous	worried
7. helmet	life vest	sunbathing

C Look at the photos. Name the activity and say if it is healthy or unhealthy.

1.

2.

3.

1. _____

2. _____

3. _____

D Use comparatives, superlatives, or expressions with *as/not as* to complete the sentences.

1. Sunbathing is _____*not as healthy*_____ (healthy) as wearing sunblock.

2. Jack is wearing a seatbelt, but Luis is not. Jack is being _____ (safe) than Luis.

3. Junk food is _____ (nutritious) fruits and vegetables.

4. It is _____ (good) for your health to exercise than to smoke.

5. Drinking alcoholic beverages and driving is _____ (bad) thing you can do.

E Answer the questions about you. Use complete sentences.

1. What do you do to stay healthy? _____

_____

2. What is one unhealthy thing you do now that you would like to stop doing? _____

_____

3. What would you like to know more about in order to stay healthy? _____

_____

43

LESSON 2

Your Health History

A Preview the article about medical histories by checking the questions you think will be answered. Then read the article.

☐ What personal information is included?   ☐ Should I describe my social history?

☐ Whose health problems do I need to describe?   ☐ What will the form look like?

☐ Where do I go for information?   ☐ What order is the information on a medical history form?

Your Personal Medical History

You will probably have to fill out a medical history form every time you go to a new doctor. It's a good idea to have this information on hand. You should start now to gather the information before you will need it.

What to do: First, you should write down all your personal information, such as your name, date of birth, and insurance policy number. Then you should list any major health-related events (immunizations, surgeries, special procedures) and the dates they occurred, and your healthcare providers over time. You should gather any paperwork related to these health events, and collect contact information for the doctors.

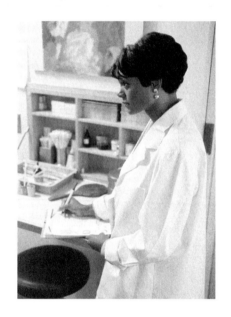

What to include: In addition to your personal information and description of specific medical events, you will usually have to list any symptoms you have now, allergies, medications you are taking, your social or lifestyle habits, and some important information about family members (siblings, parents, grandparents, and children).

B Answer the questions with complete sentences.

1. Why should you write up your personal medical history? _____

2. What are some examples of significant medical events? _____

3. For which family members should you have medical information? _____

C Look at the form. Answer the questions.

ADULT MEDICAL HISTORY FORM

1
Name: _____ Age: _____

Insurance #: _____ Date of birth: _____

CURRENT MEDICATIONS

2
Medication   Dose   How many times/day

_____

_____

3 **ALLERGIES:**

_____

4 **IMMUNIZATIONS:**

Hepatitis A _____ Hepatitis B _____ Measles _____

Rubella _____ Tetanus _____ Influenza _____

5 **MEDICAL PROBLEMS:**

Please indicate if you have had any of the following (with dates):

☐ heart disease _____ ☐ high blood pressure _____

☐ diabetes _____ ☐ cancer _____

☐ stroke _____ ☐ high cholesterol _____

☐ depression _____ ☐ alcoholism _____

FAMILY HISTORY (check family members who have had the following):

6

Medical Condition	Mother	Father	Sister	Brother	Daughter	Son	Grand-father	Grand-mother
Asthma								
Cancer								
Heart Attack								
Diabetes								
Stroke								

7 **SOCIAL HISTORY**

Do you wear a bike helmet?   ☐ Yes   ☐ No

Do you use seatbelts?   ☐ Yes   ☐ No

How do you rate your diet?   ☐ Good   ☐ Fair   ☐ Poor

Do you drink alcohol?   ☐ Yes   ☐ No   # drinks/week _____

1. In which section of the form would you write that you have diabetes? _____

2. In which section would you note that you had a tetanus shot? _____

3. In which section you indicate you are taking medication for high blood pressure? _____

4. In which section would you check that your mother had asthma? _____

D Complete the form with information about yourself.

3
LESSON

Try to improve your diet.

A Read the conversation. Write the missing words.

caffeine complaint don't exercise should you

Physician: Hello, Mr. Waters. How are _____ feeling today?

Patient: Pretty good. My only _____ is that I can't sleep very well at night.

Physician: How much _____ do you drink each day?

Patient: Well, I have a couple cups of coffee in the morning and tea in the evening.

Physician: You _____ cut down on your caffeine intake. Also, what do you do just before bedtime?

Patient: That's usually when I go to the gym. I _____ for about an hour and a half. I thought that would make me tired.

Physician: Actually, exercise can wake you up. Why _____ you try exercising earlier in the day?

Patient: Okay, I'll give it a try.

B Answer the questions.

1. What's the patient's name? _____

2. What is his problem? _____

3. What two things might be causing the problem? _____

4. What is the doctor's advice? _____

C Match the problem and advice.

Problem	Advice
1. ____ "I feel nervous a lot."	a. "I suggest you eat less junk food."
2. ____ "I get really out of breath when I walk up stairs."	b. "I think you should reduce the amount of caffeine you drink."
3. ____ "I'd really like to lose some weight."	c. "Why don't you ask the doctor about allergies?"
4. ____ "I'm going to the beach tomorrow."	d. "I recommend that you get more exercise."
5. ____ "Around this time every year, I get a stuffy nose and itchy eyes."	e. "You should wear sunblock."

D Look at the photos. Identify the problem and give advice.

1. What is the problem? _____

   What advice would you give? _____

   _____

   _____

   _____

2. What is the problem? _____

   What advice would you give? _____

   _____

   _____

   _____

★ ★

TAKE IT OUTSIDE: Interview two family members, friends, or coworkers. Ask about a health concern. Write one suggestion.

Name	One concern the person has about his/her health	Your advice
Toby	Wants to quit smoking	He should ask his doctor for help.

★ ★

LESSON 4

Giving Advice

A Look at the nutrition labels from three different cereals below.

Plain Good Oats

Nutrition Facts
Serving Size: 3/4 cup dry
Servings per container: 30

Amount Per Serving
Calories   150
Calories from fat   25

                                        % daily
Total Fat 3 g   5%
  Saturated fat 0.5g   2%
  Polyunsaturated fat 1 g
  Monounsaturated fat 1 g
Cholesterol 0mg   0%
Sodium   0%
Total Carb 27 g   9%
  Dietary fiber 4 g   15%
  Sugars 1 g
Protein 5 g

Ingredient: Rolled oats.

Sir Crunchy

Nutrition Facts
Serving Size: 3/4 cup dry
Servings per container: 17

Amount Per Serving
Calories   110
Calories from fat   15

                                        % daily
Total Fat 1.5 g   2%
  Saturated fat 0.5g   2%
Cholesterol 0mg   0%
Sodium 200 mg   8%
Total Carb 23 g   8%
  Dietary fiber 1 g
  Sugars 12 g
Protein 1 g

Ingredients: Corn flour,
sugar, oat flour, brown sugar,
partially hydrogenated oil,
salt, yellow 5 coloring, BHT (a
preservative).

Flakes of Nature

Nutrition Facts
Serving Size: 1 cup dry
Servings per container: 8

Amount Per Serving
Calories   140
  Calories from fat   10

                                        % daily
Total Fat 1 g   2%
  Saturated fat 0.5g   0%
Cholesterol 0 mg   0%
Sodium 85 mg   4%
Total Carb 30 g   9%
  Dietary fiber 10g   40%
  Sugars 6 g
Protein 13 g

Ingredients: soy grits, whole
wheat, brown rice, whole
grain oats, barley, triticale,
rye, sesame seeds, corn meal,
oat flour, honey, natural
flavors, salt.

B Check the information listed on the labels in Activity A.

☐ the size of the serving

☐ the ingredients in the product

☐ the cost of the product

☐ the amount of flour

☐ the grams of fat

☐ the total amount of carbohydrates

☐ the amount of sugar

☐ the amount of oats

☐ the amount of salt (sodium)

☐ the amount of protein

☐ the number of servings in the container

C Complete the chart with information from Activity A.

How much	Plain Good Oats	Sir Crunchy	Flakes of Nature
Calories per serving			
Size of serving			
Total fat (g)			
Sugar (g)			
Fiber (g)			
Salt/sodium (mg)			
Protein (g)			

D Read the situations below. Write your advice.

1. Your father has diabetes and needs to cut down on the amount of sugar in his diet. Which cereal would you advise he eat and why? _____

_____

2. Your sister has high blood pressure. The doctor told her to avoid salt. Which cereal would you recommend to her and why? _____

_____

3. Your best friend is trying to lose weight. She is following a low-fat diet. Which cereal do you think is best for her and why? _____

_____

4. Your daughter has been feeling tired and can't focus in the afternoons. Her doctor suggested that she eat more protein. Which cereal do you recommend and why? _____

_____

Have you had a check-up this year?

LESSON 5

A Write questions using the cues and the present perfect.

1. ever/you/be/in a car accident

   _____ ?

2. Florida/visit/you/ever

   _____ ?

3. have/all their shots/your children

   _____ ?

4. any emails/write/in the last week/you

   _____ ?

5. learn/your class/about the simple past

   _____ ?

B Complete the conversations. Use the present perfect and the cues in parentheses.

1. **A:** _____ ? (eat Chinese food)

   B: No, I haven't. But I've eaten Japanese food.

2. **A:** _____ ? (fly in an airplane)

   B: No, he hasn't. He's never even been to an airport.

3. **A:** _____ ? (ride a motorcycle)

   B: Yes, she has. She said she was afraid the whole time.

4. **A:** _____ ? (go to the dentist)

   B: Yes, they have. They went last week.

5. **A:** _____ ? (snow in April)

   B: Yes, it has. In 1923, it snowed 3 feet on April 6.

6. **A:** _____ ? (see that movie)

   B: No, we're supposed to see it tonight.

C Complete the paragraph below. Use simple past or present perfect.

Last year I _____ (1. decide) to get in shape. I _____ (2. not be) a long-distance runner then, so I _____ (3. begin) to train. I _____ (4. always like) to exercise, but I _____ (5. never enjoy) running. However, I _____ (6. run) three to five miles every day for the last nine months. In January, I _____ (7. race) for the first time. I _____ (8. come) in almost last, but I _____ (9. not mind). I _____ (10. work) hard for almost a year, and I think I _____ (11. achieve) my goal.

D Write a paragraph about a change you have made in your life. Use simple past and present perfect.

_____

_____

_____

_____

_____

_____

_____

FAMILY

LESSON

Is your child ready to go back to school?

A Check the factors that you think may influence children's health and performance in school.

- ❑ height
- ❑ weight
- ❑ how well they see
- ❑ how well they hear
- ❑ allergies
- ❑ how much they eat for breakfast
- ❑ what kind of backpack they carry
- ❑ what notebooks they have
- ❑ if their immunizations are up-to-date

B Preview the article on back-to-school health issues. Were your answers in Activity A correct? Read the article.

Health Checklist for Back-to-School

The start of school is just around the corner, so now is the time to make sure your children are ready.

Can your child see and hear well? Many children don't succeed in school because they have vision or hearing problems that haven't been treated. Make an appointment to have your child's vision and hearing tested before the start of school.

Has your child had all the required immunizations? Children are not allowed to enter school without the necessary immunizations. Make sure their immunizations are up-to-date and that you have the record.

Have you updated your emergency information? Make sure your child and the school know how to reach you or another emergency contact at all times. List all necessary phone numbers.

Have you talked to your child about any other concerns? Is your child anxious or upset about anything related to school? Give children a little time to adjust at the beginning of the year, but if it continues to be a problem, talk to a counselor at school.

Have you notified the school about other medical issues? Make sure the nurse knows what medications your child takes and about any allergies your child might have. Food allergies are especially important, because of the food in the cafeteria and brought by other children.

What are some other issues? Children who eat breakfast do better in school. Make sure that your child is not carrying a back pack that doesn't fit or is too heavy.

C   Answers the questions using information from Activity A.

1. What must children have before they can enter school?

   _____

2. What problems might affect your child's performance in school?

   _____

3. What phone numbers should you give to the school?

   _____

4. When should your child talk to the counselor?

   _____

5. What information should you give to the school nurse?

   _____

6. What is one problem you see in the picture?

   _____

★ ★

TAKE IT OUTSIDE: Interview a family member, friend, or coworker. Ask the questions below. Write their answers.

1. How many children do you have in school? _____

2. Have they all had vision and hearing tests? _____

3. Do any of your children have allergies? If so, what kind of allergies?

   _____

4. What concerns do you have about your children's health and school?

   _____

★ ★

TAKE IT ONLINE: Use your favorite search engine and enter the words "back to school health." Write down three ideas from the information you find.

_____

_____

_____

WORK

LESSON

Wellness Programs

A Answer the questions.

1. How can an employer help workers be healthier?

_____

2. Why should an employer be concerned about workers' health?

_____

B Look at the website information below. Check your answers for Activity A.

⊠ ⊟ ⊞   **WELLNESS**

- Benefits
- Employee Assistance
- Fitness Center
- Health and Safety
- Retirement
- State Employees'
- Credit Union
- Women's Resources

Wellness

As part of our commitment to hire and **retain** good workers, we offer a comprehensive wellness program. Healthy employees who are feeling well are more **effective** because they can focus better on their work assignments and their surroundings. Healthy workers are less likely to be absent and are more productive. This company believes in a **holistic** philosophy that promotes social, physical, emotional, spiritual, and mental health. Regular training activities for health include:

- Stress management workshops
- Guest speakers featuring local doctors
- Free access to fitness centers for faculty, staff, and students
- Yoga classes
- First aid classes
- Nutrition workshops
- Work/life balance seminars
- Preventing violence in the workplace
- Safety in the workplace

C Circle the answer with the closest meaning to the word in **bold**.

1. As part of our commitment to hire and **retain** good workers, we offer a comprehensive wellness programs.

   A. fire   B. keep   C. pay

2. Healthy employees who are feeling well are more **effective** because they can focus better on their work assignments and their surroundings.

   A. nervous   B. tired   C. able to complete work

3. This company believes in a **holistic** program that promotes social, physical, emotional, spiritual, and mental health.

   A. specific   B. exercise   C. whole

D Look at the different options in the wellness program on page 54. Rank the options from 1 (the most) to 9 (the least) in order of their interest to you.

_____ Stress management workshops

_____ Guest speakers featuring local doctors

_____ Free access to fitness centers for faculty, staff, and students

_____ Yoga classes

_____ First aid classes

_____ Nutrition workshops

_____ Work/life balance seminars

_____ Preventing violence in the workplace

_____ Safety in the workplace

★ ★

TAKE IT OUTSIDE: Interview a family member, friend or coworker. Write their answers.

1. What is the usual reason you miss work? _____

_____

2. What kind of health-related class would you be interested in? _____

_____

★ ★

TAKE IT ONLINE: Use your favorite search engine and enter the words "employee wellness programs." Write down one thing you learn.

_____

Practice Test

DIRECTIONS: Look at the nutrition label to answer the next five questions. Use the Answer Sheet.

Nutrition Facts
Serving Size: 9 cookies
Servings per container: about 5

Amount Per Serving	
Calories	**140**
Calories from fat	50

	% daily
Total Fat 6 g	**9%**
Saturated fat 3.5g	18%
Polyunsaturated fat 1 g	
Monounsaturated fat 1 g	
Cholesterol 25mg	**8%**
Sodium 95 mg	4%
Total Carb 21 g	7%
Dietary fiber <1 g	3%
Sugars 6 g	
Protein 2 g	

Ingredients: Wheat flour, butter, sugar, whole eggs, baking soda, nonfat milk.

1. What are *ingredients*?

  A. the number of servings

  B. the different foods that are in the product

  C. how much the package weighs

  D. the name of the product

2. How many servings are there in the package?

  A. 9

  B. 50

  C. 5

  D. 140

3. How many calories are in one serving?

  A. 9

  B. 50

  C. 5

  D. 140

4. Which ingredient is in the smallest amount?

  A. wheat flour

  B. butter

  C. eggs

  D. nonfat milk

5. Which is the largest amount in grams?

  A. total fat

  B. total carbohydrates

  C. total protein

  D. sugar

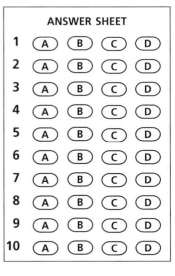

	ANSWER SHEET			
1	Ⓐ	Ⓑ	Ⓒ	Ⓓ
2	Ⓐ	Ⓑ	Ⓒ	Ⓓ
3	Ⓐ	Ⓑ	Ⓒ	Ⓓ
4	Ⓐ	Ⓑ	Ⓒ	Ⓓ
5	Ⓐ	Ⓑ	Ⓒ	Ⓓ
6	Ⓐ	Ⓑ	Ⓒ	Ⓓ
7	Ⓐ	Ⓑ	Ⓒ	Ⓓ
8	Ⓐ	Ⓑ	Ⓒ	Ⓓ
9	Ⓐ	Ⓑ	Ⓒ	Ⓓ
10	Ⓐ	Ⓑ	Ⓒ	Ⓓ

DIRECTIONS: Look at the prescription label below to answer the next five questions. Use the Answer Sheet on page 56.

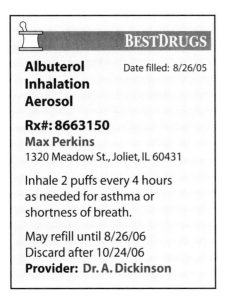

BESTDRUGS

Albuterol
Inhalation
Aerosol

Date filled: 8/26/05

Rx#: 8663150
Max Perkins
1320 Meadow St., Joliet, IL 60431

Inhale 2 puffs every 4 hours as needed for asthma or shortness of breath.

May refill until 8/26/06
Discard after 10/24/06
Provider: Dr. A. Dickinson

6. What is the number of the prescription?

A. 8/26/05

B. 8663150

C. 1320 Meadow St.

D. 10/24/06

7. Who prescribed the medicine?

A. Albuterol

B. Max Perkins

C. Dr. A. Dickinson

D. Joliet

8. What is the prescription for?

A. heart attack

B. high blood pressure

C. diabetes

D. asthma

9. Who is the patient?

A. BestDrugs

B. Max Perkins

C. A. Dickinson

D. Joliet

HOW DID YOU DO? Count the number of correct answers on your answer sheet. Record this number in the bar graph on the inside back cover.

10. How much should the patient take?

A. 2 tablets

B. 2 capsules

C. 2 bottles

D. 2 puffs

Spotlight: Reading

A Skim the article and identify the topic. Then read the article.

The article is about _____.

The New (thinner) Me
By Nancy Park

When I was a little girl, I was very thin. Then I went away to college and gained 20 pounds. I didn't exercise very much, and I ate a lot of junk food. Before that, I used to play basketball and run a lot, but in college I was too busy. After I graduated, I got a job in an office. I worked at a computer all day. At that time, my only excitement was going out to lunch. I gained ten more pounds.

Later, I met my future husband. One thing we really liked to do together was, you guessed it, go out to eat. We enjoyed all kinds of food, and soon, everyone could tell. Then I had a baby. I couldn't lose the extra 15 pounds I put on.

Last year, I noticed I was tired all the time, and I couldn't breathe very easily. I decided to get in shape. First, I talked to my doctor. She helped me work out a plan. Next, I joined a gym. I started an exercise program. I worked out three times a week. Then I changed my eating habits. I cut down on sweets and fatty foods and ate more fruits and vegetables. Because of these steps, I started to lose weight. It has taken me a year, but I'm 50 pounds lighter.

B Scan the article in Activity A to find the specific information below.

1. In college, Nancy ate a lot of _____.

2. After college, she worked in _____.

3. In her first job, she gained _____ pounds.

4. Nancy and her husband liked to _____.

5. The name of the writer is _____.

C Answer the questions about the article in Activity A.

1. What are three reasons why Nancy gained weight?

_____

_____

_____

2. What are three steps Nancy followed to lose weight?

_____

_____

_____

D Put the following events from Activity A in order from 1–7.

_____ Nancy got married.

_____ Nancy talked to her doctor.

_____ Nancy had a baby.

_____ Nancy played a lot of basketball.

_____ Nancy ate a lot of junk food.

_____ Nancy worked at a computer.

_____ Nancy exercised three times a week.

Spotlight: Writing

Using Transition Words and Phrases

A Read the timeline about Mario's life.

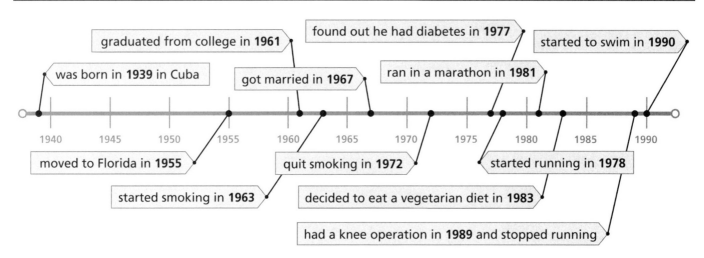

graduated from college in **1961**

found out he had diabetes in **1977**

started to swim in **1990**

was born in **1939** in Cuba

got married in **1967**

ran in a marathon in **1981**

1940 1945 1950 1955 1960 1965 1970 1975 1980 1985 1990

moved to Florida in **1955**

quit smoking in **1972**

started running in **1978**

started smoking in **1963**

decided to eat a vegetarian diet in **1983**

had a knee operation in **1989** and stopped running

B Complete the paragraph with subordinating conjunctions related to time: *when, since, while, before,* or *after.*

Mario was born in Cuba in 1939. He lived there for the next 16 years. _____ he was in Cuba, he lived with his parents. _____ he turned 16, Mario moved to Florida. _____ he graduated from college in 1961, he started smoking for the first time. _____ Mario quit smoking in 1972, he met and married his wife Doris. She didn't like his smoking. Mario always liked desserts, and he found out that he had diabetes in 1977. He decided to try to control his diabetes. _____ he started running in 1978, he didn't get much exercise. Mario has really improved his health _____ he changed his habits. He even ran in a marathon.

C Write two more sentences about Mario using subordinating conjunctions.

_____

_____

D Read the pairs of sentences. Combine the sentences using *before, after, when* or *since*. More than one answer may be correct.

1. I gained a lot of weight.
   I decided to go on a diet.

   _____

   _____

2. He starts an exercise program.
   He should talk to his doctor.

   _____

   _____

3. She hurt her arm.
   She fell off her bike.

   _____

   _____

4. We have run 3 marathons.
   We started training last year.

   _____

   _____

5. The company started wellness programs.
   Employees have been absent less.

   _____

   _____

E Write a paragraph about how you would like to change your habits to be healthier. Use at least one compound and one complex sentence.

_____

_____

_____

_____

LESSON 1

How did you make your decision?

A Combine words or phrases from each column to create collocations.

1. _____ no money   a. a warranty
2. _____ certified   b. pre-owned cars
3. _____ come with   c. down
4. _____ lease   d. or buy

B Complete the sentences with the correct form of the verb in parentheses. Use the simple past or present perfect.

1. Yesterday I _____ (lease) a truck for my business.

2. My motorcycle _____ (cost) more than my car.

3. He _____ (shop) there before.

4. We _____ never _____ (get) financing.

5. Sally _____ (buy) her dishwasher last year.

6. They _____ (pay) with a check before, but they usually use cash.

7. _____ you ever _____ (own) a car?

C Read the information about the televisions below. Answer the questions.

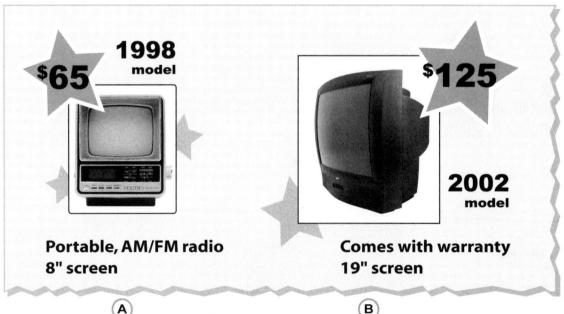

1998 model   **$65**

Portable, AM/FM radio
8" screen

A

$125   **2002 model**

Comes with warranty
19" screen

B

1. Which TV is newer? _____

2. Which TV is bigger? _____

3. Which is more expensive? _____

4. Which has a warranty? _____

5. Which one would you buy? Why? Give three reasons. _____

_____

D Look at the ads. Complete the Venn Diagram.

Adjustable desk lamp
Comes with 1 year Warranty!
60 watt bulb

$23.⁹⁹

(A)

Desk Lamp
Available in 5 colors
Uses a regular 60 watt bulb

$19.⁹⁹

SALE

Reg. $25

(B)

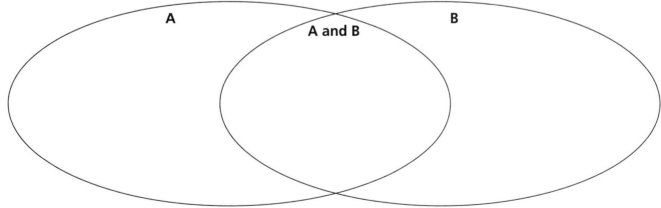

A

A and B

B

E Which lamp from Activity D would you buy and why? Give two reasons.

_____

_____

LESSON 2

This warranty is valid for 6 months.

A Scan the guarantee information to complete the sentences below.

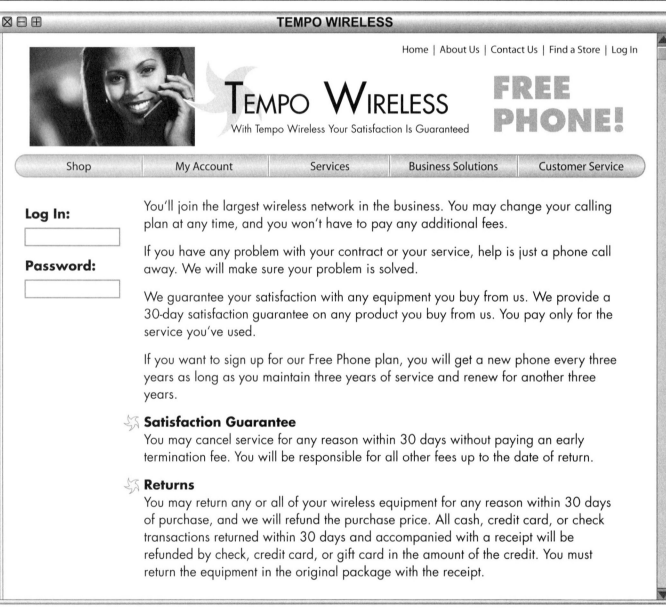

TEMPO WIRELESS

Home | About Us | Contact Us | Find a Store | Log In

TEMPO WIRELESS
With Tempo Wireless Your Satisfaction Is Guaranteed

FREE PHONE!

Shop | My Account | Services | Business Solutions | Customer Service

Log In:

Password:

You'll join the largest wireless network in the business. You may change your calling plan at any time, and you won't have to pay any additional fees.

If you have any problem with your contract or your service, help is just a phone call away. We will make sure your problem is solved.

We guarantee your satisfaction with any equipment you buy from us. We provide a 30-day satisfaction guarantee on any product you buy from us. You pay only for the service you've used.

If you want to sign up for our Free Phone plan, you will get a new phone every three years as long as you maintain three years of service and renew for another three years.

Satisfaction Guarantee
You may cancel service for any reason within 30 days without paying an early termination fee. You will be responsible for all other fees up to the date of return.

Returns
You may return any or all of your wireless equipment for any reason within 30 days of purchase, and we will refund the purchase price. All cash, credit card, or check transactions returned within 30 days and accompanied with a receipt will be refunded by check, credit card, or gift card in the amount of the credit. You must return the equipment in the original package with the receipt.

1. This company is the largest _____ network.

2. Customers may change their _____ plan at any time.

3. The company provides a _____-day satisfaction guarantee.

4. With the Free Phone Plan, customers get a free phone every _____ years.

5. If you have a problem with your service, you should _____ the company or return the equipment to the store.

6. Customers need to return the equipment in the _____ and with the _____.

B Answer the questions using information from Activity A. Write complete sentences.

1. How long is the guarantee valid?

   _____

2. Does the guarantee cover defects in the workmanship?

   _____

3. What two things do you need to do if you want a refund?

   _____

C Answer the questions about something you purchased.

1. What is one thing you bought that came with a warranty or a guarantee?

   _____

2. How long was the period of coverage?

   _____

3. Have you ever had a problem with that product? If so, what was it? Was it under a warranty or guarantee?

   _____

TAKE IT ONLINE: Use your favorite search engine to find examples of warranties on the Internet. Enter "warranty" and a cellular phone company. Complete the chart.

Type of product and brand name	Period of coverage	What is covered	What you need for a refund
Suregood Cell Phone	30 days	Defects in workmanship	Original receipt and packaging

LESSON 3

How many miles are on it?

A Put the conversation in order from 1 to 8.

_1_ Good afternoon. How can I help you today?

_____ How many miles are on it?

_____ Sure. Do you want to see a new model or are you looking for a pre-owned truck?

_____ How about this one? It's only a year old and it's a great price.

_____ I'd like to look at a small pickup truck.

_____ Just 40,000.

_____ It seems to me that that's a lot of miles on a truck that's only a year old.

_____ Pre-owned, but maybe only a year or two old.

B Answer the questions about the conversation in Activity A. Use complete sentences.

1. What is the relationship between the two people in the conversation?

   _____

2. What does the woman want?

   _____

3. Does she think the truck is a good deal? Why or why not?

   _____

4. What else should the customer ask the salesperson?

   _____

C Read the warranty for the truck in Activity A. Remember the truck in Activity A is one year old and has 40,000 miles on it. Check *True* or *False*.

NEW VEHICLE WARRANTY

The chart summarizes coverage on your new car or truck.

Type of coverage	Years/miles
Car body parts	3/30,000
Rust	3/30,000
Engine	5/50,000
Seat belts	5/50,000

The coverage is for whatever happens first. For example, if you drive 30,000 miles before you reach 3 years, you are covered up to 30,000 miles.

Your dealer will repair or replace any defective parts during the period of coverege.

Certified Pre-Owned Vehicle registered while under the New Vehicle Limited Warranty When the New Vehicle Warranty expires, the Certified Pre-Owned Vehicle Limited Warranty provides additional limited warranty for 12 months or 12,000 miles, whichever occurs first, from the date of purchase.

1. The truck is still covered by the New Vehicle Warranty if the engine fails.

   ❏ True   ❏ False

2. The truck is still covered by the New Vehicle Warranty if there are problems with the passenger side door.

   ❏ True   ❏ False

3. If the customer buys the truck, the Certified Pre-Owned Vehicle Limited Warranty will cover any rust on the truck in the next three years.

   ❏ True   ❏ False

4. The Certified Pre-Owned Vehicle Limited Warranty will provide up to one more year of coverage from the date of purchase for any problems with the seat belts.

   ❏ True   ❏ False

5. The Certified Pre-Owned Vehicle Limited Warranty will provide up to one more year of coverage for any problems with the body parts.

   ❏ True   ❏ False

★ ★

TAKE IT OUTSIDE: Go shopping for an expensive item such as a car, appliance, or computer. Ask the following questions. How much is it? Does it come with a warranty?

★ ★

Banking Needs

A Check the services you personally need in a bank.

- ☐ Home loan or mortgage
- ☐ Savings account
- ☐ Checking account
- ☐ Debit/cash card

- ☐ Student loan
- ☐ Credit card
- ☐ Currency exchange
- ☐ Money orders

- ☐ Check cashing
- ☐ Overdraft protection
- ☐ Money transfers

B Complete the sentences with phrases from Activity A.

1. When you don't have enough money to buy a house, you can get a _____ from a bank.

2. It's useful to have _____ because then you are protected if you write a check for more money than you have.

3. Banks usually offer two types of accounts: _____ and _____.

4. Some people get a _____ when they go to college to help pay tuition costs.

5. Tourists often go to a _____ when they travel to another country.

C Read the information about banks and financial institutions on the next page. Then answer the questions.

1. Which type of financial institution is run by its members?

   _____

2. Which financial institution specializes in mortgages?

   _____

3. Which financial institution offers the most services?

   _____

4. Which one offers the fewest services?

   _____

5. Which one is probably the worst option for the consumer?

   _____

⊗ ⊟ ⊞   FINANCIAL INSTITUTIONS

BANKS AND OTHER FINANCIAL INSTITUTIONS

| INSTITUTIONS | INVESTING | BUSINESS INFO | CUSTOMER SERVICE |

Commercial banks offer many services and products including savings and checking accounts, mortgages, and business and student loans. Commercial banks make a profit by providing loans and making investments.

Credit Unions are not-for-profit financial institutions. They are cooperatives run by the members. All "profits" are returned to the members in the form of lowered service fees and higher interest rates on savings accounts. They offer many of the same services as commercial banks (savings and checking accounts, loans). Some are specifically for immigrant populations, even those without documentation.

Savings and Loans started as a way to encourage saving and home ownership. They still specialize in mortgage or home loans, although they often offer savings and checking accounts too.

Currency exchanges do not accept deposits or make loans. They earn a profit by charging a fee for services such as cashing government checks or selling money orders. Their service fees are usually much higher than those of other financial institutions. Currency exchanges or check-cashing offices are often found in poorer neighborhoods.

D Look at the man in the photo. Answer the questions using complete sentences.

1. This man does not use a bank right now. What is one reason why he might not use a bank?

   _____

   _____

2. What is one problem people have when they don't use banks or credit unions?

   _____

   _____

5 **LESSON**

He goes shopping a lot.

A List seven activities you can do at a shopping mall. Use gerunds. _____

1. _____

2. _____

3. _____

4. _____

5. _____

6. _____

7. _____

B Complete the paragraph with the gerund form of words in the box. _____

compare	follow	get	look
make	pay	shop	save

Chris likes to go (1.) _____ on weekends. He usually looks in the newspaper for sales first. (2.) _____ at ads takes a little time, but it saves Chris lots of money.

(3.) _____ money is important to Chris because he would like to buy a house one day. Another way he saves money is by (4.) _____ prices at different stores.

(5.) _____ a list before going to the store helps Chris to buy only the things he needs. One thing Chris does not like is (6.) _____ with a credit card. He wants to avoid

(7.) _____ into debt. If Chris keeps (8.) _____ these money-saving steps, he will be able to buy a house soon.

C Answer the questions. Write complete sentences using gerunds.

1. What is a good way to save money?

   _____

2. How can you reduce your debt?

   _____

3. How can you get money to pay for your education?

   _____

4. What are some advantages of making a monthly budget?

   _____

5. What are some activities you could stop doing in order to save money?

   _____

D Write a paragraph about your spending habits. Use at least two gerunds.

   _____

   _____

   _____

   _____

   _____

   _____

   _____

WORK

LESSON

A W-2 Form

A Look at the sample W-2 form below.

a Control number 12378945	22222	Void ☐	For Official Use Only ▶ OMB No. 1545-0008	

b Employer identification number 12345009876	1 Wages, tips, other compensation 19,500	2 Federal income tax withheld 1592.00
c Employer's name, address, and ZIP code Dino's Pizzeria 1492 Ponce St. San Diego, CA 92101	3 Social security wages 19,500	4 Social security tax withheld 816.17
	5 Medicare wages and tips	6 Medicare tax withheld
	7 Social security tips	8 Allocated tips
d Employee's social security number 123-45-6789	9 Advance EIC payment	10 Dependent care benefits
e Employee's first name and initial Jennifer Last name House	11 Nonqualified plans	12a See instructions for box 12
	13 Statutory employee ☐ Retirement plan ☐ Third-party sick pay ☐	12b
3127 South Pleasant St. San Diego, CA 92101	14 Other	12c
		12d
f Employee's address and ZIP code		

15 State Employer's state ID number CA XXX-XXX-XXX	16 State wages, tips, etc. 19,500	17 State income tax 961.30	18 Local wages, tips, etc.	19 Local income tax	20 Locality name

Form **W-2** Wage and Tax Statement   **2006**   Department of the Treasury—Internal Revenue Service

Copy A For Social Security Administration — Send this entire page with Form W-3 to the Social Security Administration; photocopies are **not** acceptable.

For Privacy Act and Paperwork Reduction Act Notice, see back of Copy D.

Cat. No. 10134D

Do Not Cut, Fold, or Staple Forms on This Page — Do Not Cut, Fold, or Staple Forms on This Page

B Circle the best answer about the information from Activity A.

1. Who is the employer?

   A. Dino's Pizzeria   B. 1492 Ponce St.   C. Jennifer House   D. San Diego

2. Who is the employee?

   A. Dino's Pizzeria   B. 1492 Ponce St.   C. Jennifer House   D. San Diego

3. What year is this W-2 for?

   A. 2004   B. 2005   C. 2006   D. 2007

4. How much did the employee earn this year?

   A. $816.17   B. $19,500   C. $1592   D. $961.30

5. What is the employee's address?

   A. 1492 Ponce St.   B. 1492 South Pleasant St.   C. 3127 Ponce St.   D. 3127 South Pleasant St.

6. Which is the greatest amount withheld for this employee?

   A. State income tax   B. Social security tax   C. Federal income tax   D. Medicare tax

7. How much tax did the state of California withhold?

   A. $961.30   B. $15.92   C. $816.17   D. $39.00

★ ★

TAKE IT OUTSIDE: Interview a family member, friend, or coworker. Write their answers.

1. When do you usually receive your W-2 form? _____

2. How many places do you work? _____

3. When do you usually complete your tax forms? _____

4. Do you usually get a refund? _____

★ ★

TAKE IT ONLINE: Use your favorite search engine. Enter "IRS" and "forms". Write three forms you can download from the Internal Revenue Service.

_____

_____

_____

City Budgets

A Look at the pie chart to answer the questions.

Nash County's budget for 2004 was $32,000,000. The pie chart shows how the $32 million was spent.

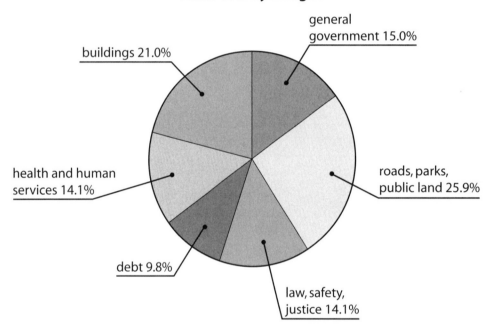

Nash County Budget

general government 15.0%

buildings 21.0%

roads, parks, public land 25.9%

health and human services 14.1%

debt 9.8%

law, safety, justice 14.1%

1. Which area did the county spend the greatest amount of money on?

   _____

2. Which two areas made up the same share of the budget?

   _____

3. What percentage of the budget did the county spend to pay back money they had borrowed?

   _____

4. What percentage of the budget was for building and maintaining buildings?

   _____

5. Which is greater, the amount spent on health and human services or on general government?

   _____

6. Approximately how much money (in dollars) did the county spend on the debt?

   _____

B Look at the table below. Complete the bar graph with information from Activity A.

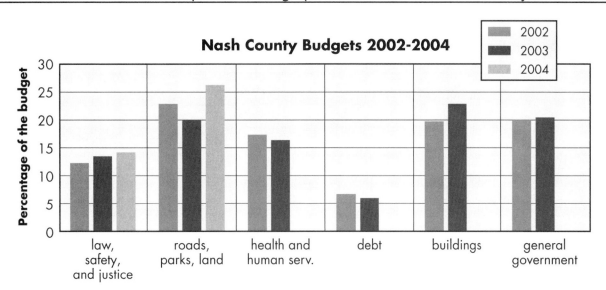

C Answer the questions about the bar graph in Activity B.

1. In which year did Nash County spend the largest percentage of the budget on buildings? _____

2. In which year did Nash County spend the lowest percentage on debt? _____

3. Which expense has increased the most over the three years? _____

4. What did Nash County spend the most on in 2003? _____

5. What did Nash County spend the least on in 2002? _____

 TAKE IT ONLINE: Use your favorite search engine to find out information about your county's budget. Enter the name of your county, "budget," and the year. Write three expenses in your county's budget and the amounts. If possible, write the percentage of the budget.

Budget category	Amount in $	Percentage of budget

★★★

TAKE IT OUTSIDE: Interview a family member, friend, or coworker. Write their answers.

1. What do you think your county spends the most money on? _____

2. What do you think is the greatest need your county has? _____

3. How have the county's needs changed over the last three years? _____

★★★

Practice Test

DIRECTIONS: Read the ad to answer the next five questions. Use the Answer Sheet.

Watches

Reg. $24.99
Now $19.99

Save 20%

Shop online for selected items.

	ANSWER SHEET			
1	A	B	C	D
2	A	B	C	D
3	A	B	C	D
4	A	B	C	D
5	A	B	C	D
6	A	B	C	D
7	A	B	C	D
8	A	B	C	D
9	A	B	C	D
10	A	B	C	D

1. What are the items on sale?

A. selected items

B. entire stock

C. watches

D. online

2. According to the ad, what is the original price of the watch?

A. $20

B. $24.99

C. $19.99

D. $200

3. What is the sale price?

A. $20

B. $19.99

C. $24.99

D. $22.99

4. How much will you save if you buy the watch on sale?

A. $20

B. $24.99

C. $19.99

D. $5.00

5. About how much would the watch cost at 40% off?

A. $14.99

B. $10.99

C. $20.00

D. $15.99

DIRECTIONS: Read the warranty below to answer the next five questions. Use the Answer Sheet on page 76.

> **Limited Warranty**
>
> Your coffeemaker is covered by the following warranty.
>
> If your coffeemaker does not work because of defects in materials or workmanship, we will repair or replace the coffeemaker. This warranty will be void if the problem is due to accident or misuse.
>
> The warranty is valid for one year from date of purchase. Purchaser must supply a receipt to prove date of purchase.

6. What product is the warranty for?

A. a vacuum

B. a car

C. a coffeemaker

D. a camera

7. What is the period of coverage?

A. a receipt

B. a refund

C. void

D. one year

8. What is NOT covered?

A. damage due to an accident

B. defects in materials

C. defects in workmanship

D. the coffeemaker

9. What will the company do if the coffeemaker is under warranty?

A. refund the money

B. repair the coffeemaker

C. replace the coffeemaker

D. both B and C

10. What does the customer need to give the company?

A. the receipt with date of purchase

B. his telephone number

C. the original package

D. the receipt and original package

HOW DID YOU DO? Count the number of correct answers on your answer sheet. Record this number in the bar graph on the inside back cover.

Spotlight: Reading

A Write the main idea for each paragraph below.

1. A new law should make you a little nervous about writing a check. It used to take a couple of days for your check to clear. That meant that if you had insufficient funds, you could write a check today, deposit the money tomorrow, and the check would still be good. Now, however, because of a new law, banks don't have to send the original check to the customers' home banks. They now can send and accept digital, or computerized, versions of the check. This means that customers might bounce a check if they are counting on a two-day lag to get that check covered.

Main idea: _____

2. The death of a spouse is perhaps the most upsetting time in anyone's life. The surviving husband or wife must make many changes in his or her life. There are many important financial decisions to make, and it can be a time of great financial stress. After the death of a spouse, survivors should put off making any major financial decisions, such as buying or selling a house. They should make sure they know of any benefits, such as life insurance. Also, survivors should make a monthly budget to account for sources of income and expenses.

Main idea: _____

3. Fly Right Airlines has announced a new destination in the tropics. Starting October 18, the airline will fly to the Bahamas from Atlanta twice a day. This will be a low-cost flight at only $109 one way. Fly Right is hoping that passengers will consider Fly Right when making vacation plans. This is the first time that Fly Right has offered a low-cost fare in a market where there is no competition.

Main idea: _____

B Look at the advice below. Write a paragraph and include the information.

How to Manage Student Loans

• Keep a list of loans.

• Know how much you owe.

• Consolidate (combine) loans, so you only have to pay one.

• Shop around for low interest rates.

• Stick to a budget.

• Try to pay more each month.

• Repaying loans is hard, so you should not get angry if it takes a long time.

_____

_____

_____

_____

_____

_____

C Write a main idea of the paragraph you wrote in Activity B.

Main idea: _____

Spotlight: Writing

A Read the paragraph below. Then complete the outline.

    Sometimes you can have too much of a good thing. Think about the last time you went to an all-you-can-eat buffet. After the second or third trip to the food line, you probably realized that you were a little full and maybe didn't really want that next helping. Or maybe you remember a birthday party when you invited so many friends that you couldn't even say hello to everyone. What about that time you went to the beach? The sun was shining, the beach was beautiful ... You spent too much time in the sun and got a terrible sunburn. That may be when you realized that after a certain point, you can have too much.

Main idea: _____

    Example 1: _____
    Detail: _____

    Example 2: _____
    Detail: _____

    Example 3: _____
    Detail: _____

B Write three pieces of advice you would give someone about saving money.

1. _____

2. _____

3. _____

C Choose one piece of advice and create a cluster diagram for your ideas.

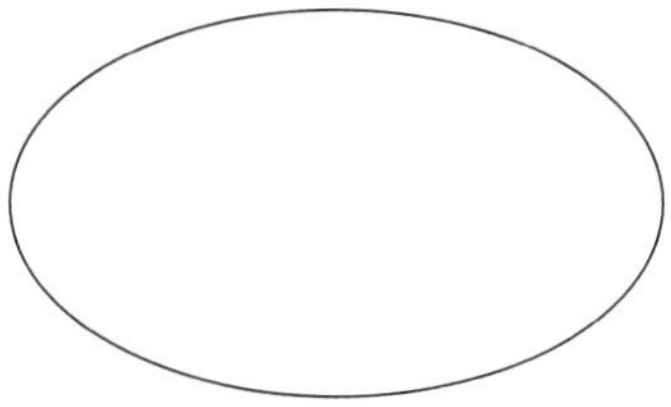

D Write an outline for a paragraph about the advice you diagrammed in Activity C.

Main idea: _____

Reason 1: _____
Detail: _____

Reason 2: _____
Detail: _____

Reason 3: _____
Detail: _____

E Use your outline to write a paragraph explaining your advice.

_____

_____

_____

_____

_____

_____

LESSON

It's a hazard!

A Look at the pictures. Identify the workplace safety equipment. Write the words from the box under the pictures.

| coveralls | gloves | fire helmet | hard hat | safety goggles | safety visor |

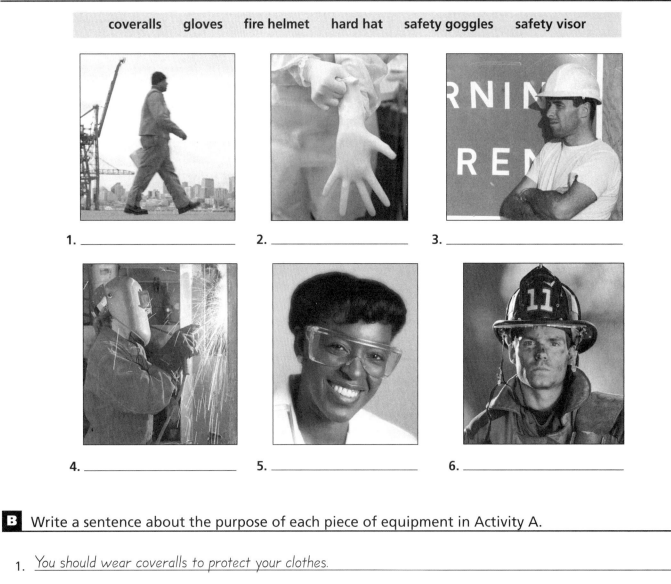

1. _____

2. _____

3. _____

4. _____

5. _____

6. _____

B Write a sentence about the purpose of each piece of equipment in Activity A.

1. *You should wear coveralls to protect your clothes.* _____

2. _____

3. _____

4. _____

5. _____

6. _____

C Read the memo.

MEMO

To: All Employees
From: Lilia Banks, Vice President
Re: Workplace Safety

In an effort to improve safety in the workplace, we are asking employees on all shifts to observe the following rules.

1. Employees should wear safety goggles at all times when they are working in the production area. Sparks from the machines can injure eyes.
2. Do not eat or drink in the work area. Spills can cause falls and can damage the machinery.
3. Employees in Shipping and Receiving must wear hard hats when working in the loading dock area.

D Write questions to ask about the memo. Then answer the questions you wrote.

1. Who _____?

   Answer: _____

2. When _____?

   Answer: _____

3. Why _____?

   Answer: _____

4. Where _____?

   Answer: _____

E Match the appropriate preventive measure to each potential hazard below.

Preventive Measure	**Hazard**
1. _____ Wear safety goggles	a. when you are working near dangerous fumes or smoke.
2. _____ Don't eat and drink in the work area	b. so chemicals don't get in your eyes.
3. _____ Wear a gas mask	c. to protect your clothing.
4. _____ Keep hands away from machinery	d. or you could cut your finger.
5. _____ Use earplugs	e. because spills can cause falls.
6. _____ Wear coveralls	f. so the loud machines don't hurt your hearing.

LESSON **2**

This is an emergency!

A Check the situations below that you think are emergencies.

- ☐ You fractured a finger.
- ☐ There is a fire in a trash can.
- ☐ You saw someone steal a car.
- ☐ A thunderstorm is coming.
- ☐ You got a dent in your car door.
- ☐ You saw a bad car accident.

- ☐ Your sister has a heart attack.
- ☐ You are locked out of your house.
- ☐ You have a sharp object in your eye.
- ☐ Someone robbed you.
- ☐ Your spouse is unconscious.
- ☐ You heard an explosion.

B Complete the sentence with your definition of *emergency.*

An emergency is _____

_____

C Look at the signs below. Write the letter of the sign next to the potential emergency.

A.

B.

C.

D.

E.

1. _____ Someone could get a bad shock.

2. _____ A fire could start.

3. _____ Someone could fall down.

4. _____ These materials are toxic.

5. _____ A train may cross the road and hit a car.

D Answer the questions. Use complete sentences.

1. Have you ever been in or witnessed an emergency situation? _____

2. What was the emergency? _____

3. Who was involved? _____

4. What did you do? _____

E Write a paragraph about an emergency you witnessed or you experienced. Use your answers from Activity D.

_____

_____

_____

_____

_____

_____

_____

_____

F Circle the correct answer.

1. I have to buy a new computer. I was the victim of a _____.
   A. robbery   B. rob   C. robbed

2. There was a gas leak at the factory. They thought something might _____.
   A. explosion   B. explode   C. explosive

3. She has a terrible rash. She thinks she touched something _____.
   A. toxin   B. intoxicate   C. toxic

4. A hurricane is coming, so the governor ordered an _____.
   A. evacuation   B. evacuate   C. evacuated

5. It was so hot yesterday. Matt had heat _____.
   A. exhaustion   B. exhaust   C. exhaustive

6. I saw a car accident. Three people were _____.
   A. injury   B. injure   C. injured

LESSON 3

I won't do it again.

A Match the employee's responses to the supervisor's questions. Write the letter on the line.

Hector Lopez (supervisor):

1. _____ How's your eye?

2. _____ Can you tell me what you got in your eye?

3. _____ When did it happen?

4. _____ How did that happen?

5. _____ Did you have safety goggles on?

6. _____ Why not? You know it's a rule.

7. _____ Did you fill out an accident report?

Tim Johnson (employee):

a. I was repairing some wires and they caught on fire.

b. It's better, thanks.

c. No, I didn't.

d. I forgot to get them before I worked on the wires. Sorry. I'll be more careful in the future.

e. Not yet. I'll do that right away.

f. Smoke and dust particles.

g. Yesterday, around 3:00.

B Complete the accident report for the incident in Activity A. Use today's date on the form.

ACCIDENT REPORT
Name of employee injured: _____
Date of injury: _____   Time of injury: _____
Body part injured: _____
Type of injury: _____
How did the injury happen: _____
_____
_____
Name of supervisor: _____
Date of report: _____

C Look at the picture below. Pretend you are the injured person. Answer the questions.

1. What happened?

   _____

2. How did it happen?

   _____

3. What did you injure?

   _____

4. How could you have prevented the accident?

   _____

   _____

D Answer the questions about yourself.

1. Have you ever had an accident at work or at school?

   _____

2. What happened?

   _____

3. What did you injure?

   _____

4. What did you do?

   _____

5. What could you do so you don't have an accident like that again?

   _____

★ ★

TAKE IT OUTSIDE: Interview a family member, friend, or coworker. Ask the questions in Activity D. Write a paragraph about the accident.

_____

_____

_____

_____

_____

★ ★

LESSON 4

First Aid

A The United States Department of Labor publishes information about injuries and illnesses that keep people home from work. Look at the graph and answer the questions.

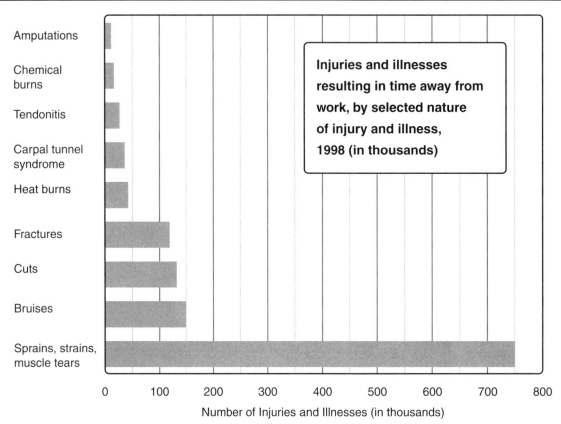

Injuries and illnesses resulting in time away from work, by selected nature of injury and illness, 1998 (in thousands)

Number of Injuries and Illnesses (in thousands)

1. About how many people missed work in 1998 because of sprains, strains, and muscle tears?
   A. 100,000
   B. 750,000
   C. 750
   D. 100

2. About how many people missed work because of chemical burns?
   A. less than 50,000
   B. more than 50,000
   C. more than 100,000
   D. about 100,000

3. Which injury caused the most people to be absent from work?
   A. cuts
   B. bruises
   C. heat burns
   D. sprains, strains, and tears

4. Which injury of the four below caused the fewest number of people to be absent?
   A. cuts
   B. bruises
   C. heat burns
   D. sprains, strains, and tears

B Read the instructions. Answer the questions.

FIRST AID

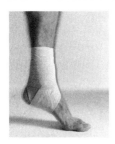

Sprains, strains and tears
- Apply cold packs or a small bag of ice wrapped in a cloth (30 minutes on, 30 minutes off) to reduce swelling.
- Wrap the joint with a supporting bandage.
- Keep the affected limb elevated.

Bruises
- Apply cold compresses or an ice pack.
- If bruise is on an arm or leg, elevate the limb.
- After 24 hours, apply a warm wet compress.

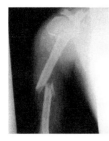

Fractures
- If the fracture is severe or open (broken bone coming through a cut in the skin), call 911.
- If it is not severe, take the victim to a hospital or doctor's office.
- Do not move the injured body part. Try to keep it immobile.

1. Which injuries benefit from putting ice on them?

   _____

2. For which injury do you have to see a doctor immediately?

   _____

3. What helps reduce swelling?

   _____

4. When should you elevate an arm or leg?

   _____

5. How long should you keep an ice pack on a strain?

   _____

5
LESSON

I wasn't paying attention.

A Read the information in the box below. Complete the sentences with either the simple past or the past continuous.

> Use the simple past in the *when* clause.
> Use the past continuous in the *while* clause.
> EXAMPLE: *I was eating when he called. He called while I was eating.*

1. I _____ (drive) down Park Street when I _____ (see) the accident.

2. Ali _____ (come) to the house while Mary _____ (study).

3. While we _____ (eat), two men _____ (break) into the apartment.

4. Sara _____ (walk) to school when it _____ (start) raining.

5. The students _____ (listen) to the teacher when the fire alarm _____ (ring).

6. When you _____ (call), I _____ (take) a shower.

7. I _____ (play) soccer when I _____ (break) my foot.

8. She _____ (not look) when the ball _____ (hit) her.

9. When they _____ (arrive), Jack _____ (talk) to the police.

10. He _____ (not breathe) when the paramedics _____ (get) there.

B Answer the questions about you. Use the past continuous.

1. What were you doing at 9 P.M. last night?

_____

2. What were you doing at this time of year two years ago?

_____

3. Think about an accident or other emergency that you witnessed. What were you doing at the time?

_____

90

4. Think about an injury that you have had. What were you doing when you were injured?

   _____

5. Have you ever had a bad fall? What were you doing when you fell?

   _____

C Complete the conversations. Use the cues.

1. **A:** _____ you _____ (break) your arm?
   What _____? (happen)

   B: I _____ (paint) the porch, and I _____
   (fall) off the ladder.

2. **A:** I can't come to work today. I _____ (sprain) my ankle.

   B: Oh no. How _____ (happen)?

   A: Julia and I _____ (dance). I _____ (trip) over the rug.

3. **A:** Will is in the hospital. He _____ (be) in an accident yesterday.

   B: That's terrible. What kind of accident?

   A: He _____ (ride) his bicycle when a car _____ (hit) him.

4. **A:** 911. What's the emergency?

   B: I want to report an accident. Someone _____ (fall) out the window.

   He _____ (wash) the windows when he _____ (slip).

FAMILY

LESSON

Knowing what to do in an Emergency

A Preview the website information in Activity B to find the main idea.

1. What is the main idea?

   A. You are ready for emergencies.

   B. You can get ready for emergencies by doing certain things.

   C. Emergencies

   D. Change your batteries.

B Read the information from a government website (www.citizencorps.gov) about how you can be safer. Check the things you already do.

ARE YOU READY?

❑ 1. Check and change the batteries in your smoke alarms and replace all alarms that are more than 10 years old.

❑ 2. Make sure you know where your local fire department, police station, and hospital are and post a list of emergency phone numbers near all the telephones in your home.

❑ 3. Organize and practice a family fire drill—make sure your children know what your smoke detector sounds like, what to do if it goes off, and where to meet outside the house.

❑ 4. Locate the utility mains (gas, electricity, and water) for your home in case you have to leave, and be sure you know how to turn them off manually.

❑ 5. Create an emergency plan for your household, including your pets. Decide where your family will meet if a disaster does happen: 1) right outside your home in case of a sudden emergency like a fire, and 2) outside your neighborhood in case you can't return home—ask an out of town friend to be your "family contact" to relay messages.

❑ 6. Check expiration dates of all over-the-counter medications—discard all that are expired and replace any that are routinely needed.

❑ 7. Make sure all cleaning products and dangerous objects are out of children's reach.

C Write the number of the tasks from the reading under the appropriate headings on the chart. You may write a task in more than one place.

To be ready for a fire	To prevent medical emergencies	To be ready to evacuate

D Answer the questions about you.

1. When did you buy your smoke detector(s)? _____

2. Where is the closest hospital to your home? _____

3. What medications do you usually use? _____

4. Where will your family or friends meet outside the neighborhood if there is an emergency? _____

_____

★ ★

TAKE IT OUTSIDE: Interview someone who is not in your family. Ask the questions in Activity D. Write a paragraph in the space below and give that person suggestions about how he or she can get ready for an emergency.

_____

_____

_____

_____

_____

★ ★

TAKE IT ONLINE: Use your favorite search engine to find out more about "family emergency plans." Write down two things you learn.

1. _____

2. _____

COMMUNITY

LESSON

Getting Out of a Building

A Read the information from www.ready.gov.

1. Use available information to evaluate the situation. Note where the closest emergency exit is.

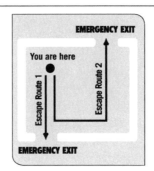

2. Be sure you know another way out of the building in case your first choice is blocked.

3. Take cover under a desk or table if things are falling.

4. Move away from file cabinets, bookshelves or other things that might fall.

5. Face away from windows and glass. Move away from exterior walls.

6. Determine if you should stay put, "shelter-in-place" or get away. Listen for and follow instructions from authorities.

7. Take your emergency supply kit, unless there is reason to believe it has been contaminated.

8. Do not use elevators.

9. Stay to the right while going down stairwells to allow emergency workers to come up the stairs into the building.

B Match the sentence to the correct box from Activity A. Write the number on the line.

_____ When you go downstairs, walk on the right.

_____ Don't stand by objects that may fall.

_____ Listen for directions on what to do.

_____ Know where the closest emergency exit is.

_____ Use the stairs.

_____ Take all emergency supplies with you.

_____ Don't stand by windows.

_____ If things may fall on you, get under furniture.

_____ Know where all the exits are.

C Answer the questions in complete sentences.

1. How many times a week are you in a big building?

_____

2. How often do you use an elevator?

_____

3. Where are the closest emergency exits at your school or work?

_____

★★

TAKE IT OUTSIDE: Interview a family member, friend, or coworker. Ask the questions in Activity C. Answer the questions below.

1. Which of you is in a big building more often? _____

2. Who uses an elevator more often? _____

★★

TAKE IT ONLINE: Use your favorite search engine and enter the name of your city or state and "community emergency resources." Write down two things you learn.

_____

_____

Practice Test

DIRECTIONS: Look at the accident report below to answer the next five questions. Use the Answer Sheet.

ACCIDENT REPORT

(1) Name of employee injured: _Alina Mann_

(2) Date of injury: _12/02/06_   Time of injury: _12:30 p.m._   (3)

(4) Body part injured: _right hand_
Type of injury: _cut_

How did the injury happen: _Alina Mann was operating the printing machine_
(5) _when the machine jammed. She tried to free the jam, but she forgot to_
turn the machine off.

(6) Name of supervisor: _Terry Jones_
Date of report: _12/03/06_

1. Who got hurt?
   A. Alina Mann
   B. Terry Jones
   C. right hand
   D. cut

2. What was she doing at the time of the accident?
   A. She was printing.
   B. She was cutting.
   C. She was operating a machine.
   D. She was trying to free the jam in the machine.

3. Where on the form do you write the time of the accident?
   A. Part 1
   B. Part 2
   C. Part 3
   D. Part 4

4. Where do you write the date the form was completed?
   A. Part 2
   B. Part 3
   C. Part 5
   D. Part 6

5. What did she hurt?
   A. her right hand
   B. her left hand
   C. her cut
   D. a jam

ANSWER SHEET

	A	B	C	D
1	A	B	C	D
2	A	B	C	D
3	A	B	C	D
4	A	B	C	D
5	A	B	C	D
6	A	B	C	D
7	A	B	C	D
8	A	B	C	D
9	A	B	C	D
10	A	B	C	D

DIRECTIONS: Read the article about first aid to answer the next five questions. Use the Answer Sheet on page 96.

Head injuries

1. Check for bleeding. If there is severe bleeding, apply pressure with a sterile bandage to stop the bleeding.

2. If the person is conscious and alert, put an ice pack on the injury to reduce swelling. Make sure you wrap the ice or ice pack in a cloth before you put it on the skin.

3. Watch the person with the head injury for 24 hours. If there are any signs of concussion, call a doctor immediately. A concussion is a bruise to the brain. If breathing or skin color changes, or if the injured person appears confused and disoriented, call a doctor.

6. What should you do if there is bleeding?

A. Call 911.

B. Apply an ice pack.

C. Apply pressure with a sterile bandage.

D. Wrap ice in a cloth.

7. What should you do to the ice pack before you put it on the skin?

A. Call 911.

B. Call your doctor.

C. Wrap the ice pack in a cloth.

D. Apply pressure.

8. What is a concussion?

A. a cut

B. an injury to the brain

C. a bruise on the head

D. pressure

9. When should you call the doctor?

A. if there is a cut

B. if the injured person's breathing changes

C. if you need ice

D. if there is swelling

10. How long should you watch the injured person?

A. for one day

B. for 2 hours

C. for 2 weeks

D. until they fall asleep

HOW DID YOU DO? Count the number of correct answers on your answer sheet. Record this number in the bar graph on the inside back cover.

Spotlight: Reading

A Think about a job you had or would like to have. List three adjectives that describe that job.

_____

_____

_____

B Survey the story on page 99. Answer the questions.

1. What job do you think this story is about?

   _____

2. What are two adjectives that you think describe this job?

   _____

C Write three questions that you think the story might answer. Then read the story and answer the questions you wrote.

1. _____?

Answer: _____

2. _____?

Answer: _____

3. _____?

Answer: _____

D Reread the story. List four qualities you think a paramedic should have.

_____   _____

_____   _____

The Life of a Paramedic

I have been a paramedic for several years, and I really like my job most of the time. To become a paramedic, you need two years of specialized training. I completed a certificate program at the local community college. I learned a lot, but school couldn't prepare me completely for the life of a paramedic which is exciting, rewarding, and stressful.

One thing I really like about my job is that it is not routine. We travel all over the city, and you never know what you will be doing from one hour to the next. We treat all kinds of medical emergencies. I learn something new every day.

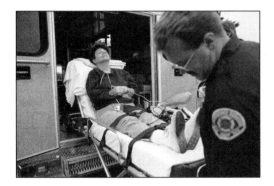

Being a paramedic is very rewarding. I've always wanted a career in medicine because I like to help other people and I enjoy science. As a paramedic, I help people all the time: drivers in car accidents, elderly people who have heart attacks, and children who fall on the playground. My patients can't always thank me, but I'm happy when I can assist them.

The major disadvantage of the job is the stress. Paramedics deal with life and death situations all the time. Although it is rewarding to help someone, we aren't always successful. Sometimes a patient dies. We also have to work very quickly, and that can be stressful, too. We deal with people who are hurt and in trouble, and sometimes they are very stressed, too.

E Write a paragraph about the job you chose to describe in Activity A. Use the story as a model.

_____

_____

_____

_____

_____

_____

_____

_____

Spotlight: Writing

A Read the paragraph below and take notes in the Venn Diagram.

Hurricanes or blizzards? Take your pick. No matter where you live, you will probably have bad weather some time. In the northeastern United States, summers are often pleasant, but winters can be cold and snowy. Some winter storms can dump up to several feet of snow. Temperatures can go below 0° Fahrenheit (–18° Celsius). In the southeastern United States, winters are nice and relatively warm, but summers bring their own danger. Hurricanes, with wind speeds over 100 miles (161 kilometers) an hour and a lot of rain, frequently hit Florida and nearby states. Both areas of the country experience weather emergencies and may lose power during a bad storm.

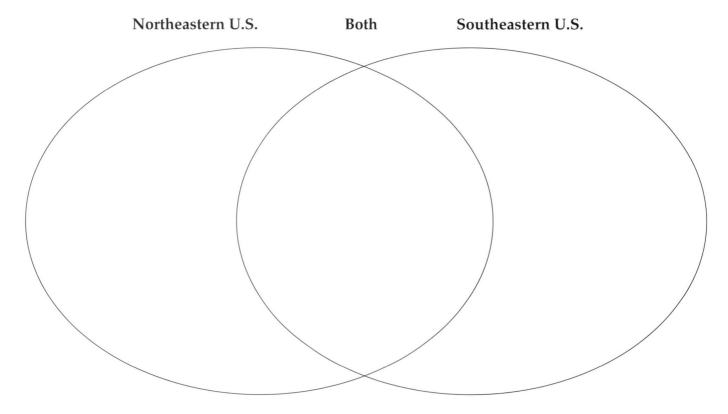

Northeastern U.S.   Both   Southeastern U.S.

B Think about two places you have lived. Take notes in the Venn Diagram below.

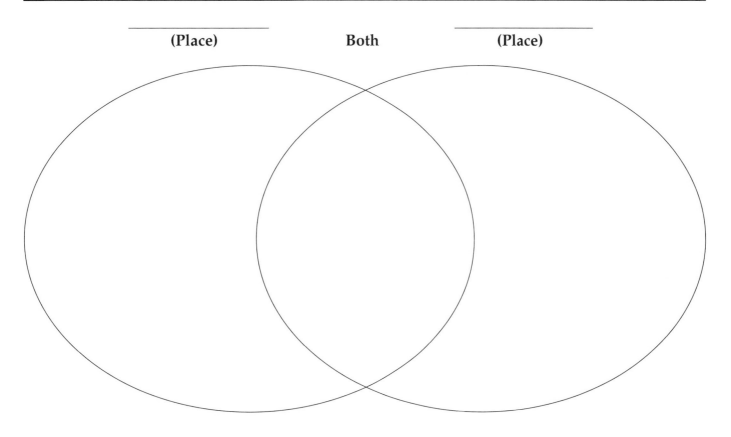

_____   Both   _____
      (Place)   **(Place)**

C Write a paragraph comparing the two places you chose for Activity B.

_____

_____

_____

_____

_____

_____

_____

_____

_____

_____

_____

LESSON

What makes a community good?

A Look at the table below that compares the qualities of two cities in the United States. Answer the questions.

Feature		Rancho Santa Margarita, CA	Naperville, IL
Weather	High temperature	82.3°F	86.8°F
	Low temperature	47.2°F	14.2°F
Financial	Median income*	$84,000	$94,000
	Sales tax	7.75%	6.75%
	Auto insurance	$795	$748
	Home price	$309,000	$252,000
Culture	Libraries (within 30 miles)	22	75
	Museums	2	13
	Pro sports teams	2	5
Airports	(within 30 miles)	2	2
Crime			
	Personal crime risk **	31	12
	Property crime risk	31	22
Education	(within 30 miles)		
	Colleges, universities	10	33
	Junior colleges, technical institutes	36	59
	Student-teacher ratio in public schools (K–12)	20	13

*national average: $43,527   **based on 100 average, lower is better   Table adapted from http://money.cnn.com/best/bplive/details

1. What is the high temperature in Rancho Santa Margarita? _____

2. What is the low temperature in Naperville? _____

3. What is the median income per year in the United States? _____

4. Is the median income in Naperville higher or lower than the national average? _____

5. How many libraries are within 30 miles of Naperville? _____

6. How many museums are within 30 miles of Rancho Santa Margarita? _____

7. Where is the personal crime risk higher, in Rancho Santa Margarita or Naperville? _____

8. Which community has the higher number of colleges? _____

9. Which community has the lower student to teacher ratio? _____

B Rank the following community features in order of their importance to you.

1 = very important   10 = not important.

_____ a strong economy with a lot of jobs   _____ active community members

_____ good public schools   _____ a clean environment (no graffiti, litter)

_____ low crime   _____ good public transportation

_____ close to colleges and universities   _____ friendly people

_____ low housing prices   _____ good city services, like garbage collection

_____ lots of public parks

C Answer the questions about you.

1. Which community in Activity A would you rather live in? Why?

_____

2. What makes the community you chose more attractive to you?

_____

3. What are three good features of your city or town?

_____

4. What are three things that your city or town could improve?

_____

★ ★

TAKE IT OUTSIDE OR ONLINE: Choose three features listed in the table in Activity A. Go to the library or online and find out the information for your city or town. Write three things you learn.

_____

_____

_____

★ ★

2 LESSON

Littering is prohibited.

A You work with a neighborhood group. The photos below show problems in your local park. Complete the flyer below and prohibit these behaviors.

1.

2.

4.

3.

5.

NOTICE TO ALL PARK VISITORS

We are proud of our park. Help to make it more enjoyable. Please observe the following rules:

1. _____

2. _____

3. _____

4. _____

5. _____

Thank you very much for your help.

B Look at the signs below. Write the rule and give the reason for the rule.

1

2

3

4

RULE	REASON FOR RULE
1. _____	1. _____
2. _____	2. _____
3. _____	3. _____
4. _____	4. _____

I'm sorry, officer.

A Read the conversation below. Complete the sentences with words from the box.

| apologize | apply | license | posted | sign | speeding |

Park officer: I need to see your fishing license and some identification, please.

Mark Todd: Here's my driver's _____. Do we need fishing licenses here? I didn't know that.

Park officer: Yes, you do. In fact, it's _____ on the sign at the park entrance.

Mark Todd: I'm sorry, officer. We didn't see the _____. Where can we get a license?

Park officer: You can _____ online or go to the Fish and Game office downtown. I'm afraid you can't fish until you have a license, and I'm going to have to give you a citation.

Mark Todd: Again, I _____. Of course, we won't fish until we get the license.

Park officer: I think you may have also been _____. You can see there's a speed limit for boats coming through this area.

B Look at Mark Todd's online application for a fishing license.

DIVISION OF FISH AND WILDLIFE

Fishing in New Jersey
New Jersey Division
of Fish and Wildlife

FISHING LICENSE APP.

Check Off	License Name	Description	Fee	Min Age	Max Age
✔	Annual Fishing	Required to fish in fresh water for anyone who has been a resident of NJ for at least six months. No license required for residents under 16 years of age.	22.50	16	64
☐	Senior Fishing	Issued to residents between 65 and 69 years old for fresh water fishing. Residents 70 years or older may fish without a license with proof of age.	12.50	65	69
✔	Trout Stamp	Required in addition to the regular fishing license, of every resident between 16 and 69 years of age who shall take or attempt to take trout from any fresh waters of the state. Trout Stamps are valid for the calendar year (Jan-Dec).	10.50	16	69

Enter Applicant Information:

Name: Mark   J   Todd

Soc. Sec. #: 123-45-6789

E-mail: marktodd9999@versit.net

Street: 23 South Park Dr.

City: Monmouth   State: NJ   Zip: 07724

County: Atlantic

Phone: 732-555-7888

Date of Birth: 04/19/50   Sex: ● Male   ○ Female

Eye Color: Brown   Hair Color: Gray

C Answer the questions. Use complete sentences.

1. How old is Mark Todd? _____

2. Can he get a senior fishing license? _____

3. How much will he pay for his fishing license? _____

4. What color is his hair? _____

5. What will the total cost be for Mark? _____

107

LESSON 4

Is it a good law?

A Read the news articles and complete the chart.

Smokers Get A Break

The City Council passed a new, less-restrictive smoking ordinance yesterday, giving smokers a break.

The new ordinance replaces one passed last year which prohibited smoking in all public buildings. This new ordinance allows smoking in bars and restaurants but prohibits children under 18 years of age from entering without a parent.

Businesses will pay $300 to get permission to allow smoking on the premises. The ordinance takes effect on Sept. 1.

Noise Out, Quiet In

The Town Council voted Tuesday to reduce noise levels within town limits. Beginning June 30, it will be illegal to operate electronic equipment such as radios, CD players, and loudspeakers loud enough to be heard 20 feet away between 10 p.m. and 7 a.m.

In addition, the new ordinance prohibits operating a device if the sound vibration can be felt 20 feet away. This means that drivers cannot play car stereos so loud that it rocks the car next to them at a traffic light.

Violators can be fined up to $2,500 or face 180 days in jail.

Ordinance Limits Dogs and Cats

A new city ordinance takes effect next month that will limit the number of dogs and cats an owner can have. Under the new ordinance, you can have up to four dogs, up to five cats, and no more than six animals total.

Council member Jake Lamont said, "It's just not healthy for the animals or for the people when there are too many pets in a house."

The City Council passed this measure to prevent several problems, including the neglect and mistreatment of the animals and unsanitary conditions in neighborhoods.

	Smokers Get A Break	Noise Out, Quiet In	Ordinance Limits Dogs and Cats
What was the problem?			
What does the ordinance prohibit?			
Who passed the law?			
When does it take effect?			

B Reread the articles in Activity A. List two pros (reasons for) and two cons (reasons against) of each law.

	Pros	Cons
Less restrictive smoking ban		
Noise control ordinance		
Pet restrictions		

C Write a paragraph about which law in Activity A you think is best and why.

_____

_____

_____

_____

_____

D Look at the following situations. Check how you think they should be handled.

Situations	By law	Within the family	Nothing should be done
1. Parent hitting child			
2. Dogs going to the bathroom on the street			
3. Drivers talking on cell phones			
4. Students eating in the classroom			
5. Children smoking cigarettes			
6. Cars going through red lights			
7. People begging for money on the street			
8. Young children seeing R-rated movies			

E Answer the question.

What is one situation in your community that you think is a problem? How can you help solve it?

_____

_____

_____

LESSON 5

Exercise your right to vote.

A Read the editorial from the newspaper. Underline the infinitives. Write them on the chart.

Exercise Your Right

Next Tuesday, we will have an opportunity to exercise one of our most important rights as citizens—the right to vote. As citizens, we not only have the right, we have the duty to vote. This election will determine who will represent us at a local, state, and national level. We may need to work or to go to school that day. We might want to avoid the lines at the voting places. We may be frustrated with our political leaders and wish to stay home.

Yes, there are good reasons to stay home on Tuesday, but there are even better reasons to go to the polls. Go early to miss the lines, get a babysitter to take care of the kids, or call your boss to explain you'll be late, but go and vote. It's important to participate in government by voting.

After certain verbs	After nouns	To express purpose	After adjectives in *It* expressions

B Express your opinion. Complete the sentences with an infinitive or an infinitive phrase.

1. If you want to be a good citizen, it's important _____.

2. If you want to be a good parent, it's a good idea _____.

3. Some actions are wrong. You should refuse _____.

4. If your boss asks you _____, you shouldn't do it.

5. People should read _____.

C Look at the photos below. Complete the sentences with infinitives that express your ideas.

1. Some teens hang out on the streets _____.

2. In order to get teenagers off the streets, parents need _____

   _____.

3. When you're homeless, it's difficult _____.

4. In order to help the homeless, the city government needs _____

   _____.

5. The city should make it illegal _____

   _____.

D Write an editorial about one of the problems in Activity C. Use at least three infinitives.

_____

_____

_____

_____

_____

UNIT 6: Community

How do you discipline your children?

A Read the following article.

DISCIPLINING CHILDREN

When you were a child, did your dad or mom spank you when you did something wrong? Nowadays fewer and fewer children get hit on their bottoms as punishment. An increasing number of parents prefer to use forms of discipline other than physical punishment. In fact, punishing your children by hitting them may be considered child abuse in some places. Fortunately, there are many other ways to get your children to behave.

It's important to tell your children what you want in a positive way. For example, "Use your words," instead of "Don't hit your brother," tells your child what behavior is expected and reinforces that communication is better than violence.

Parents should also set clear limits. It's impossible to set rules for everything, so you should think about what is most important. Usually parents create rules to prevent people from getting hurt, protect property, and encourage respect for others.

When a child does something wrong, parents should respond appropriately. For example, if your son comes in too late at night, you might make him stay in for the rest of the week. Sometimes just separating the child from the rest of the family or the activity for a little while can be an effective punishment. This is often called giving the child a "timeout."

Check *True* or *False.* Then correct the false statements.

1. More American parents are spanking their children as punishment.

   ☐ True   ☐ False

2. According to the article, "Don't fight" is an example of a good rule.

   ☐ True   ☐ False

3. American parents discipline their children the same way as they did 50 years ago.

   ☐ True   ☐ False

4. According to the article, rules about safety are not very important.

   ❏ True   ❏ False

5. One effective punishment is to send the child away from the rest of the family for a few minutes.

   ❏ True   ❏ False

6. It's important to tell children what behavior you expect from them.

   ❏ True   ❏ False

B   Answer the questions about you.

1. What is one mistake you made as a child?

   _____

2. Were you punished for the mistake? If so, how?

   _____

3. In your culture or family, how are children disciplined when they do something wrong?

   _____

4. What is one thing that surprises you about how parents discipline children in this country?

   _____

★ ★

TAKE IT OUTSIDE: Interview a family member, friend, or coworker. Ask the questions in Activity B. Take notes. Write three sentences summarizing their answers.

_____

_____

_____

★ ★

TAKE IT ONLINE: Use your favorite search engine to find out about what is considered child abuse in this country. Enter the phrase "definition of child abuse." Write down three things that are considered abusive.

_____

_____

_____

UNIT 6: Community

I've got a problem at work.

A Preview the information in Activity C. What do you think it will be about?

❏ Supervisors

❏ Solving problems

❏ Getting promotions

B Read the sentences below. Choose the meaning of the **bold** word. Circle the answer.

1. Problems and complaints in the workplace can be solved quickly and fairly if the parties involved follow certain guidelines. You can get information about resolving **disputes** by calling the Human Relations Office at 555-9000.

   A. relationships

   B. disagreements

   C. solutions

   D. guidelines

2. One way to solve disputes is through **mediation**. In the mediation process, both parties involved in the dispute meet with a trained mediator. The mediator is from outside the department. He or she listens to both sides of the argument and helps the parties come to an agreement.

   A. a problem-solving process

   B. a complaint

   C. a supervisor

   D. training

3. If mediation fails to solve the problem, an employee can file a **grievance**.

   A. a problem

   B. mediation

   C. a complaint

   D. a supervisor

4. Employees who file a grievance cannot be subject to **retaliation**. A supervisor may not give an employee who made a complaint more difficult work, an inconvenient schedule, or otherwise punish the employee for complaining.

   A. punishment

   B. extra money

   C. promotion

   D. complaining

C Read the information. Check *True* or *False*.

⊠ ⊟ ⊞   **State Dept. of Human Resources**

State Department of Human Resources

Home Page | About Us | Empoyment Opportunities | Feedback | Contact Us

HOW TO HANDLE DISPUTES IN THE WORKPLACE

Problems and complaints in the workplace can be solved quickly and fairly if the parties involved follow certain guidelines. You can get information about resolving disputes by calling the Human Relations Office at 555-9000.

One way to solve disputes is through mediation. In the mediation process, both parties involved in the dispute meet with a trained mediator. The mediator is from outside the department. He or she listens to both sides of the argument and helps the parties come to an agreement.

If mediation fails to solve the problem, an employee can file a grievance. A grievance is a formal complaint, and it may move through three levels of management. When you file a grievance, the person who hears the grievance must make a decision about how to resolve the problem within 30 days.

Employees who file a grievance cannot be subject to retaliation. A supervisor may not give an employee who made a complaint more difficult work, an inconvenient schedule, or otherwise punish the employee for complaining.

1. You should file a grievance before trying mediation.   ☐ True   ☐ False
2. The mediator is usually the supervisor of the employees.   ☐ True   ☐ False
3. A grievance is a complaint about a problem.   ☐ True   ☐ False
4. A supervisor can punish an employee for making a complaint.   ☐ True   ☐ False

D Answer the questions.

1. Have you ever had problems with someone at work or known someone who had? If so, what was the problem?

   _____

2. How was the problem solved? _____

★ ★

TAKE IT OUTSIDE: Interview a family member, friend, or coworker. Write their answers.

1. Who can you talk to at work to get help with a problem? _____

2. What can you do if you have a problem with a supervisor? _____

★ ★

TAKE IT ONLINE: Use your favorite search engine to find out about types of discrimination in the workplace. Enter "types of workplace discrimination."

Practice Test

DIRECTIONS: Refer to the application form to answer the next five questions. Use the Answer Sheet.

Enter Applicant Information

| | First | MI | Last |

① Name: _____

② Soc. Sec. #: _____

③ E-mail: _____

④ Street: _____

City: _____ State: _____ Zip: _____

County: _____

Phone: _____

⑤ Date of Birth: _____ Sex: _____

⑥ Eye color: _____ Hair color: _____

Check license desired: ⑦
- ☐ regular fishing
- ☐ senior
- ☐ child

1. On which part of the application would you put your e-mail address?
   A. Part 1
   B. Part 2
   C. Part 7
   D. Part 3

2. Where would you write your eye color?
   A. Part 1
   B. Part 6
   C. Part 4
   D. Part 2

3. What information do you need?
   A. your county
   B. your country
   C. your driver's license number
   D. your occupation

4. How many types of licenses are there?
   A. 1
   B. 2
   C. 3
   D. 4

5. Which part lists your date of birth?
   A. Part 1
   B. Part 3
   C. Part 5
   D. Part 7

ANSWER SHEET

1	Ⓐ Ⓑ Ⓒ Ⓓ
2	Ⓐ Ⓑ Ⓒ Ⓓ
3	Ⓐ Ⓑ Ⓒ Ⓓ
4	Ⓐ Ⓑ Ⓒ Ⓓ
5	Ⓐ Ⓑ Ⓒ Ⓓ
6	Ⓐ Ⓑ Ⓒ Ⓓ
7	Ⓐ Ⓑ Ⓒ Ⓓ
8	Ⓐ Ⓑ Ⓒ Ⓓ
9	Ⓐ Ⓑ Ⓒ Ⓓ
10	Ⓐ Ⓑ Ⓒ Ⓓ

DIRECTIONS: Read the article below to answer the next five questions. Use the Answer Sheet on page 116.

WALK TO HELP MOM CHANGE DOG LAW

A 20–mile fund-raising walk will take place on Saturday to raise money for the mother of a six-year-old boy killed by pit bulls in March. Bobby Taylor was bitten by his neighbor's dogs as he played outside in his yard. Bobby died as a result of the bites. Now his mother, Kim Taylor, is trying to get the City Council to prohibit pit bulls and other dangerous breeds of dog.

Taylor has collected 2000 signatures for her petition. She is raising funds for flyers, TV ads, and newspaper ads that will explain the law and ask others to help. City Council members will consider the petition next year.

6. What is happening on Saturday?

   A. a walk

   B. a City Council meeting

   C. a new law

   D. a petition

7. Why does Kim Taylor want to prohibit pit bulls?

   A. They're noisy.

   B. They're playful.

   C. They're dangerous.

   D. They're friendly.

8. Who will make the decision about the dogs?

   A. petition

   B. the City Council

   C. Kim Taylor

   D. neighbors

9. Who is Bobby Taylor?

   A. Kim's brother

   B. Kim's husband

   C. Kim's father

   D. Kim's son

10. When will City Council vote?

   A. on Saturday

   B. in March

   C. next year

   D. tonight

HOW DID YOU DO? Count the number of correct answers on your answer sheet. Record this number in the bar graph on the inside back cover.

Spotlight: Reading

A Reread the article. Paraphrase each of the nine sentences.

Exercise Your Right

Next Tuesday we will have an opportunity to exercise one of our most important rights as citizens—the right to vote. As citizens, we not only have the right, we have the duty to vote. This election will determine who will represent us at a local, state and national level. We may need to work or to go to school that day. We might want to avoid the lines at the voting places. We may be frustrated with our political leaders and wish to stay home.

Yes, there are good reasons to stay home on Tuesday, but there are even better reasons to go to the polls. Go early to miss the lines, get a babysitter to take care of the kids, or call your boss to explain you'll be late, but go and vote. It's important to participate in government by voting.

_____

_____

_____

_____

_____

_____

_____

_____

_____

B Read the article. Paraphrase each of the six sentences.

NEIGHBORHOOD CRIME WATCH GROUPS

The neighborhood crime watch movement started more than 30 years ago. Through neighborhood crime watch organizations, local officials, law enforcement officers, and members of the community work together to keep a neighborhood safe. This approach has helped reduce problems in high-crime areas. The idea is a simple one—neighbors keep an eye on the neighborhood, reporting any suspicious activity to police. Members of a neighborhood crime watch group do not take action; they just observe and report to authorities.

For information about how to start your own neighborhood crime watch program and for resources to help your group succeed, go to our website.

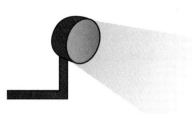

Spotlight: Writing

A Reread the articles from the unit and read the summaries. None of the summaries are perfect. Each one has a problem. Explain what the problem is.

Smokers Get A Break

The City Council passed a new, less-restrictive smoking ordinance yesterday, giving smokers a break.

The new ordinance replaces one passed last year which prohibited smoking in all public places. This new ordinance allows smoking in bars and restaurants but prohibits children under 18 years of age from entering without a parent.

Businesses will pay $300 to get permission to allow smoking on the premises. The ordinance takes effect on Sept. 1.

Summary: Yesterday, the city council voted on a new smoking ordinance. The new ordinance will be easier on smokers. Last year, the city council passed another smoking ordinance, and it said that no one could smoke in public places. The new law begins on Sept. 1.

Problem: _____

Noise Out, Quiet In

The Town Council voted Tuesday to reduce noise levels within town limits. Beginning June 30, it will be illegal to operate electronic equipment such as radios, CD players, and loudspeakers loud enough to be heard 20 feet away between 10 P.M. and 7 A.M.

In addition, the new ordinance prohibits operating a device if the sound vibration can be felt 20 feet away. This means that drivers cannot play car stereos so loud that it rocks the car next to them at a traffic light.

Violators can be fined up to $2,500 or face 180 days in jail.

Summary: The town council passed a new ordinance to prohibit any radios, CD players, or loudspeakers. Also, drivers cannot play car stereos.

Problem: _____

B Reread the article. Write a summary for the article.

Ordinance Limits Dogs and Cats

A new city ordinance takes effect next month that will limit the number of dogs and cats an owner can have. Under the new ordinance, you can have up to four dogs, up to five cats, and no more than six animals total.

Council member Jake Lamont said, "It's just not healthy for the animals or for the people when there are too many pets in a house."

City Council passed this measure to prevent several problems, including the neglect and mistreatment of the animals and unsanitary conditions in a neighborhood.

Summary: _____

_____

_____

_____

C Find a news story in your local newspaper or online. Answer the questions.

1. What happened? _____

2. Where? _____

3. Who was involved? _____

4. When did it happen? _____

5. How or why? _____

D Write a summary of the article you found. Be sure to include your answers from Activity C.

_____

_____

_____

_____

_____

LESSON 1

What makes a workplace good?

A Read the article.

WHAT'S THE RIGHT CAREER FOR YOU?

Trying to decide what career is best for you can be difficult. Many career counselors use the Holland Code to help students decide on a career. The Holland Code was developed by Dr. John Holland to describe personality and job types. There are six categories.

Realistic people like to work with their hands, work outside, solve problems, and build or fix things. Firefighting is a realistic career.

Investigative people like to work wih numbers or science. They are interested in ideas, like to solve problems, and are often good with computers. Scientists and computer programmers are investigative professionals.

Conventional people like detail-oriented and organized workplaces. They may like to work with math, finance, and computers. They also like to work with information. Accounting is a conventional occupation.

Artistic people are creative and often like casual work environments. They like to sing, dance, act, write, and communicate with others. Actors and designers are artistic people.

Enterprising people often like business or politics. They are confident and like to persuade others. They like to speak in public and lead others. Sales and law are enterprising fields.

Social people enjoy helping others and in the community. They like to talk and get along well with others. Teaching and nursing are social careers.

B Complete the sentences with information from the article in Activity A.

1. A singer is an example of a(n) _____ professional.

2. A(n) _____ person might like to be a mechanic.

3. Accountants like a workplace that is detail-oriented and _____.

4. A sales manager probably likes to _____ in public.

5. Teachers like to _____ others.

6. A scientist is interested in _____.

C Look at the photos. Identify the job and write the category from Activity A.

1.

Job: _____

Category: _____

2.

Job: _____

Category: _____

3.

Job: _____

Category: _____

4.

Job: _____

Category: _____

5.

Job: _____

Category: _____

6.

Job: _____

Category: _____

LESSON 2

Does the job have good benefits?

A Read the situations below. Write the most important job benefit each person needs.

dental insurance	flex time	telecommuting
on-site basic skills courses	paid family leave	

1. Rob and Greta can't have children of their own. They want to adopt a little girl. They have filled out all the paperwork, and they think the adoption will happen in the next year or two. Rob is looking for a new job right now, but he wants to take some time off when they adopt a child. Rob should look for a job with

_____.

2. Lily is a writer. She writes training materials for big companies. Lily likes a quiet work environment, so she can really focus on her writing. She would like to work from home. When she looks for work, she tries to find a job that allows

_____.

3. Aziz arrived in this country two months ago. He has one job now in a factory, but he wants to get a part-time job, too. He sends money to his family in his home country. The problem is Aziz doesn't know much English and needs it in his job. He doesn't have time to take classes. He needs a job that offers

_____.

4. Eddie has three children, and they all wear braces. He has good health care benefits at his current job, but he is thinking about applying for a job that offers

_____.

5. Terry and Nick have four small children. Nick works from 8 to 5 every day. Terry wants to get a job, but she would like to work flexible hours. She doesn't want the kids to spend long hours in day care. Terry is looking for a job with

_____.

B Complete the following conversations. Use the cues in parentheses.

1. **Mary Brown:** I'm excited about your offer, but first I'd like to know more about the benefits.

   _____? (offer/health care benefits)

   Joe Smith: Yes, we do. We offer a great medical insurance plan with low co-pays for routine visits.

2. **Mary Brown:** _____? (what/family leave policy)

   Joe Smith: Six weeks paid leave and four weeks unpaid.

3. **Mary Brown:** _____? (on-site basic skills courses)

   Joe Smith: Yes, GED and Adult ESL.

4. **Mary Brown:** _____? (provide/tuition reimbursement)

   Joe Smith: No, we don't. The company does offer some on-site training though.

5. **Mary Brown:** _____? (what/other benefits)

   Joe Smith: Other benefits include an on-site gym and on-site day care.

C Write three questions you would ask about benefits during a job interview.

_____

_____

_____

I'm calling about the ad for a photographer.

LESSON 3

A Put the conversation in order from 1 to 10.

_____ **Ms. Nevins:** It starts at $30,000, but it depends on experience.

_1_ **Katia:** Hello, I'm calling about the ad for a writer.

_____ **Ms. Nevins:** At least two years at a magazine or newspaper.

_____ **Katia:** What should I do if I want to apply?

_____ **Ms. Nevins:** Yes, how can I help you?

_____ **Katia:** Would you know the salary range?

_____ **Ms. Nevins:** Sure. Go to our website and click on "Contact us" and then "Rose Nevins."

_____ **Katia:** And what kind of experience are you looking for?

_____ **Ms. Nevins:** You can send two copies of your resume and a cover letter to 1300 South Street, attention Rose Nevins.

_____ **Katia:** Can I send them electronically?

B Answer the questions.

1. What position is Katia interested in? _____

2. What is the lowest salary possible? _____

3. How many years of experience are required? _____

4. What are two ways Katia can send her resume? _____

_____

C Unscramble the words to write questions about a job position.

1. salary/would/the/you/starting/know

   _____

2. the name/could/me/of the open position/you/tell

   _____

3. the supervisor's/I/ask/may/name

   _____

4. you/the duties/can/me/tell

   _____

5. the qualifications/tell/you/me/could

   _____

D Answer the questions in Activity C about a job you have or know about.

1. _____
2. _____
3. _____
4. _____
5. _____

★ ★

TAKE IT OUTSIDE OR ONLINE: Look in the newspaper or at an online job bank. Find a job that you might be qualified for. Write three questions you would ask about the job before applying.

1. _____
2. _____
3. _____

Find the contact information for the job. Get the answers.

★ ★

LESSON 4

Résumés

A Read the résumé below and identify the type (chronological or functional).

Hana Nasser | 11510 South Lake Dr. Atlanta, GA 30318
(770) 555-5482   hanacooks@global.net

JOB OBJECTIVE:

Work as pastry chef with a catering company

WORK EXPERIENCE:

Rosie's Bakery
Shift supervisor, 2003–present
- Head baker, 1st shift
- Supervised baking assistants
- Managed supply inventory
- Catered at large parties

Bread For It
Baker, 2002–2003
- Sole bread baker
- Developed new recipes
- Helped manager with inventory

Lebanon Café
Waitress, 2000–2002
- Waited tables
- Operated the cash register
- Assisted in the kitchen

Résumé type: _____

B Answer the questions about the résumé in Activity A.

1. Whose résumé is this? _____

2. What kind of job does she want? _____

3. Where does she live? _____

4. How can someone contact her? _____

5. How many years has she been in the food business? _____

6. Does she have supervisory experience? _____

7. Does she have experience working with customers? _____

8. What kinds of food do you think she cooks? _____

C Complete the application form below for Hana Nasser. Use the information from Activity A.

Catered to You!
Catering Company
Job Application

Name: _____

Address: _____

Telephone No: _____ Email: _____

Position you are applying for: _____

WORK EXPERIENCE: (start with your most recent job)

1. Position: _____ Dates: _____ Company: _____

Duties: _____

_____

_____

D Complete the interview between a manager of a catering company and Hana Nasser. Use the information from Activity A.

1. **Manager:** So why are you applying for a job with "Catered to You"?

   Hana: _____

2. **Manager:** We make a lot of cakes and pies. Have you been a pastry chef before?

   Hana: _____

3. **Manager:** What kind of experience do you have working with customers?

   Hana: _____

4. **Manager:** Often our customers have special requests. How flexible are you about trying new things?

   Hana: _____

5. **Manager:** We deal with lots of supply companies. What experience do you have managing inventory?

   Hana: _____

6. **Manager:** Of course, we have to travel to different locations all the time, and sometimes the pastry chef prepares on-site. How do you feel about working with a team at a site?

   Hana: _____

5
LESSON

If the company closes, she'll go back to school.

A Write answers to the questions below. Use real conditionals.

1. **Interviewer:** What will you say if we offer you the job right now?

   Applicant: *If you offer me the job right now, I* _____

2. **Interviewer:** When will you be able to start if you get the job?

   Applicant: _____

3. **Applicant:** If I want to find out more about this position, whom can I talk to?

   Interviewer: _____

4. **Applicant:** What should I do if I want to get a promotion within a year?

   Interviewer: _____

5. **Applicant:** How could the company help me if I want to get an advanced degree?

   Interviewer: _____

6. **Interviewer:** How will you manage your responsibilities if you are still taking classes?

   Applicant: _____

7. **Interviewer:** If you are asked back for another interview, whom may we contact as a reference?

   Applicant: _____

8. **Applicant:** If I have any more questions, whom should I call?

   Interviewer: _____

B Look at the flowchart. Complete the real conditional sentences with either an *if* or *result clause*.

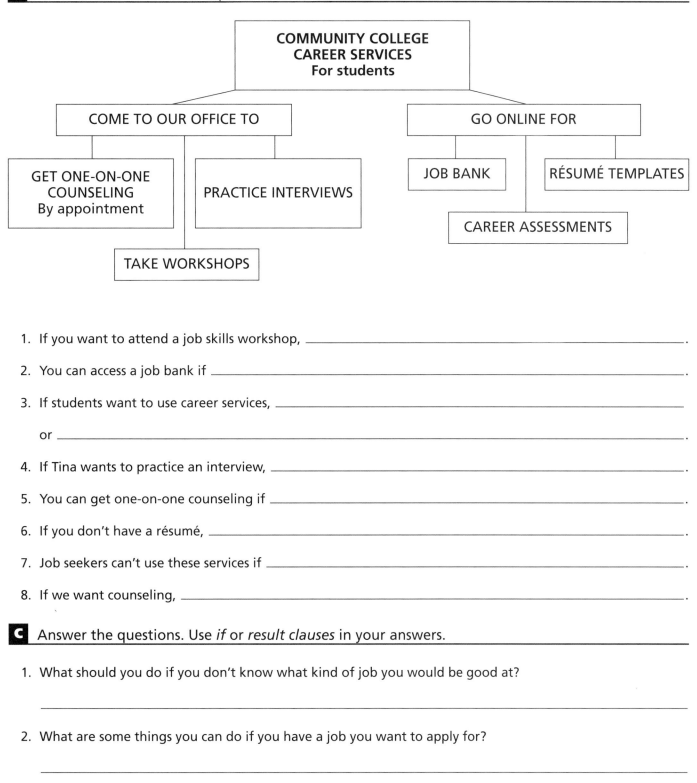

1. If you want to attend a job skills workshop, _____.

2. You can access a job bank if _____.

3. If students want to use career services, _____

   or _____.

4. If Tina wants to practice an interview, _____.

5. You can get one-on-one counseling if _____.

6. If you don't have a résumé, _____.

7. Job seekers can't use these services if _____.

8. If we want counseling, _____.

C Answer the questions. Use *if* or *result clauses* in your answers.

1. What should you do if you don't know what kind of job you would be good at?

   _____

2. What are some things you can do if you have a job you want to apply for?

   _____

FAMILY

LESSON

How much time can you take off?

A Read the information about the Family and Medical Leave Act (FMLA). This law allows employees to take leave for serious medical problems.

Family and Medical Leave Act (FMLA)
Frequently Asked Questions and Answers

Q: *How much leave am I entitled to under FMLA?*
A: If you are an "eligible" employee, you are entitled to 12 weeks of leave for certain family and medical reasons during a 12-month period.

Q: *Which employees are eligible to take FMLA leave?*
A: Employees are eligible to take FMLA leave if they have worked for their employer for at least 12 months, and have worked for at least 1,250 hours over the previous 12 months, and work at a location where at least 50 employees are employed by the employer within 75 miles.

Q: *Does the law guarantee paid time off?*
A: No. The FMLA only requires unpaid leave. However, the law permits an employee to elect, or the employer to require the employee, to use accrued paid leave, such as vacation or sick leave, for some or all of the FMLA leave period. When paid leave is substituted for unpaid FMLA leave, it may be counted against the 12-week FMLA leave entitlement if the employee is properly notified of the designation when the leave begins.

Q: *Can the employer count leave taken due to pregnancy complications against the 12 weeks of FMLA leave for the birth and care of my child?*
A: Yes. An eligible employee is entitled to a total of 12 weeks of FMLA leave in a 12-month period. If the employee has to use some of that leave for another reason, including a difficult pregnancy, it may be counted as part of the 12-week FMLA leave entitlement.

Q: *Who is considered an immediate "family member" for purposes of taking FMLA leave?*
A: An employee's spouse, children (son or daughter), and parents are immediate family members for purposes of FMLA. The term "parent" does not include a parent "in-law". The terms son or daughter do not include individuals age 18 or over unless they are "incapable of self-care" because of mental or physical disability that limits one or more of their "major life activities" as those terms are defined in regulations issued by the Equal Employment Opportunity Comission (EEOC) under the Americans With Disabilities Act (ADA).

Source: http://www.dol.gov/elaws/esa/fmla/faq.asp

B Answer the questions.

1. How much time off can you get for family or medical leave? _____

2. Does your employer have to pay you for this time? _____

3. Do adult children usually count as immediate family? _____

4. Can you use sick leave instead of FMLA leave? _____

5. Which employees are guaranteed FMLA leave? _____

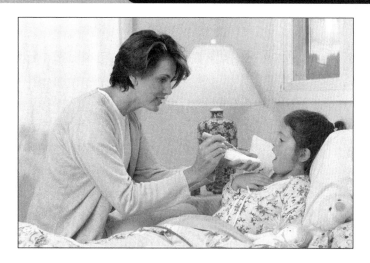

C Answer the questions.

1. How many days were you sick last year? _____

2. How many days did you miss work or school because you were sick? _____

3. How many days did you take care of someone else who was sick? _____

4. Does anyone in your household have a serious medical problem? If yes, who takes care of him or her?

_____

★ ★

TAKE IT OUTSIDE: Interview a family member, friend, or coworker. Write their answers.

1. What work benefit do you think is the most helpful to an employee with a family?

_____

2. Which benefits, if any, do you get from your job that help your family?

_____

3. If you could change one thing about your job to help your family life, what would it be?

_____

★ ★

TAKE IT ONLINE: Use your favorite search engine and enter the words "family and work issues." Make sure you use the quotation marks around the words. Write down three topics you think are interesting.

_____

_____

_____

COMMUNITY

LESSON

What are my rights?

A Read the government information on employment discrimination (Title VII).

⊠⊟⊞   **FEDERAL EQUAL EMPLOYMENT OPPORTUNITY LAWS**

The U.S. Equal Employment Opportunity Commission

FEDERAL EQUAL EMPLOYMENT OPPORTUNITY LAWS (EEOC)

Under federal laws, it is illegal to discriminate in any aspect of employment, including:
- hiring and firing;
- compensation, assignment, or classification of employees;
- transfer, promotion, layoff, or recall;
- job advertisements;
- recruitment;
- testing;
- use of company facilities;
- training and apprenticeship programs;
- fringe benefits;
- pay, retirement plans, and disability leave; or
- other terms and conditions of employment.

Discriminatory practices under these laws also include:
- harassment on the basis of race, color, religion, sex, national origin, disability, or age;
- retaliation against an individual for filing a charge of discrimination, participating in an investigation, or opposing discriminatory practices;
- employment decisions based on stereotypes or assumptions about the abilities, traits, or performance of individuals of a certain sex, race, age, religion, or ethnic group, or individuals with disabilities; and
- denying employment opportunities to a person because of marriage to, or association with, an individual of a particular race, religion, national origin, or an individual with a disability. Title VII also prohibits discrimination because of participation in schools or places of worship associated with a particular racial, ethnic, or religious group.

Employers are required to post notices to all employees advising them of their rights under the laws EEOC enforces and their right to be free from retaliation. Such notices must be accessible, as needed, to persons with visual or other disabilities that affect reading.

B Check *True* or *False*.

1. An employer can refuse to hire you if you are too disorganized.
   ❑ True   ❑ False

2. An employer can fire you if you join a new religion.
   ❑ True   ❑ False

3. Under federal law you cannot be fired because you are too old.
   ❑ True   ❑ False

4. It's okay for employers to treat you differently because English is not your first language.
   ❑ True   ❑ False

5. Although an employer can't refuse to hire someone of another race, the employer can look for new hires at places where people of that race are not likely to be.
   ❑ True   ❑ False

★ ★

TAKE IT OUTSIDE: Interview a family member, friend, or coworker. Write their answers.

1. Has anyone ever treated you unfairly because of your national origin, race, religion, or gender? If so, how?

   _____

2. In your workplace, do men and women hold the same jobs?

   _____

3. Do you think employment practices in this country are generally fair?

   _____

4. What advice would you give to someone who is looking for work in this country for the first time?

   _____

★ ★

TAKE IT ONLINE: Use your favorite search engine and enter "EEOC" or go to www.eeoc.gov. Choose one of the types of discrimination (age, disability, equal pay, national origin, pregnancy, race, religion, sex, sexual harassment). Go to the link and write down three things you learn.

_____

_____

_____

REVIEW

LESSON

Practice Test

DIRECTIONS: Refer to the job application form to answer the next five questions. Use the Answer Sheet.

Carter Company

Job Application Form
(PLEASE PRINT)

(1) Name: _Daniel Gomez_

Address: _1655 Maple Street Martinsburg, West Virginia 25401_

(2) Telephone No: _304-555-8822_   email: _ddgogomez@global.net_

Position you are applying for: _Accountant_

(3) **WORK EXPERIENCE:** (start with your most recent job)

1. Position: _____ Dates: _____ Company: _____

Duties: _____

_____

(4) 2. Position: _____ Dates: _____ Company: _____

Duties: _____

_____

(5) **EDUCATION:**

School	Dates attended	Graduated	Degree

1. On what part of the application would you list your most recent job?

  A. Part 1   B. Part 2   C. Part 3   D. Part 4

2. Where would you say what job you are applying for?

  A. Part 1   B. Part 2   C. Part 3   D. Part 4

3. Where would you list the schools you attended?

  A. Part 5   B. Part 4   C. part 3   D. Part 2

4. Who is the applicant?

  A. accountant   B. Daniel Gomez   C. Carter Company   D. ddgogomez

5. Who is the employer?

  A. accountant   B. Daniel Gomez   C. Carter Company   D. ddgogomez

	ANSWER SHEET			
1	A	B	C	D
2	A	B	C	D
3	A	B	C	D
4	A	B	C	D
5	A	B	C	D
6	A	B	C	D
7	A	B	C	D
8	A	B	C	D
9	A	B	C	D
10	A	B	C	D

DIRECTIONS: Read the job listings to answer the next five questions. Use the Answer Sheet on page 136.

New Listings:

WBNC, Trenton, NJ
WRITER
> **Duties:** will write news stories, write live updates, contact sources by phone, help producer develop graphics.
> **Qualifications:** College degree preferred. News writing experience preferred. Excellent writing skills, good command of English, attentive to details, good computer skills, ability to gather information quickly, ability to work on a team and meet deadlines.

KNRR, San Jose, CA
PRODUCTION ASSISTANT
> **Duties:** write, help producer, schedule guests for shows, research story ideas.
> **Qualifications:** college degree, excellent writing skills, good organizational skills, creative, strong computer skills. Must have excellent communication skills and be able to deal with pressure.

WQAP, Tallahassee, FL
ACCOUNT ASSISTANT
> **Duties:** Sell advertising time to advertising agencies and retail businesses. Call on community contacts to develop new business. Develop and maintain business contacts.
> **Qualifications:** Minimum three years sales experience preferred. Ability to meet goals. Excellent oral and written communication skills, strong mathematical ability, Florida driver's license and personal transportation required.

KUPS, Seattle, WA
CAMERA OPERATOR
> **Duties:** Operate camera at the station and on location with news teams.
> **Qualifications:** Minimum two years' experience.

6. Which job requires a driver's license?

A. writer
B. production assistant
C. account assistant
D. camera operator

7. Which job is in San Jose?

A. writer
B. production assistant
C. account assistant
D. camera operator

8. Which job requires two years' experience?

A. writer
B. production assistant
C. account assistant
D. camera operator

9. Where is the writing job?

A. San Jose
B. Tallahassee
C. Seattle
D. Trenton

10. What is a duty of the account assistant?

A. operate a camera
B. schedule guests
C. develop graphics
D. call on businesses

HOW DID YOU DO? Count the number of correct answers on your answer sheet. Record this number in the bar graph on the inside back cover.

Spotlight: Reading

A Read the story below and answer the questions. Write one piece of evidence from the story that supports your answer.

Ben is the owner of a small business in Pittsburgh. His company makes and sells specialty T-shirts. Ben has 10 to 12 employees at any one time. His wife is the bookkeeper, and his son does the marketing. Ben wants to provide his employees with good benefits, but he worries about health insurance. The cost of providing quality health insurance for just a dozen employees is very high, and Ben doesn't know if he can afford it anymore. This issue is very important to Ben. In the next election, he plans to vote for the candidates that he thinks will do the most to make health care manageable.

1. Do you think Ben has a stressful job? _____

   What is the **evidence** for your answer? _____

2. Do you think Ben wants to be a good boss? _____

   Evidence: _____

3. Do you think Ben is an American citizen? _____

   Evidence: _____

4. Do you think Ben's family dislikes his job? _____

   Evidence: _____

B Read the job listing below. Then read the inference and check *True* or *False*. Write a piece of evidence that supports your answer.

> **Administrative Assistant**
>
> **Duties:** Maintain business and community contacts, help director with meetings, schedule appointments and interviews, assist with the budget.
> **Qualifications:** Four years experience in office setting, preferably in the media, excellent computer skills, can deal with the public in a professional manner, ability to handle stress, college degree preferred.

1. The administrative assistant should be good with numbers. ☐ True ☐ False

   Evidence: _____

2. You won't have to use the computer in this position. ☐ True ☐ False

   Evidence: _____

3. This position is probably relaxing. ☐ True ☐ False

Evidence: _____

4. The administrative assistant needs to be good with people. ☐ True ☐ False

Evidence: _____

5. This position is probably in television or at a magazine or newspaper. ☐ True ☐ False

Evidence: _____

C Read the letter below.

Dear Human Resource Director:

I am writing in response to your ad for an account assistant in the *Houston Tribune* on May 3. I would enjoy the opportunity to meet with you to discuss this position.

As you can see in the enclosed résumé, I have worked in sales and marketing for three years since I graduated from the University of Texas. I have excellent computer and communication skills. I am able to deal with pressure, meet deadlines, and manage multiple responsibilities at one time.

Sincerely,
Rebecca Andersson

D Answer the questions with complete sentences.

1. Do you think the writer is organized? Why or why not?

_____

2. What duties do you think the account assistant might have? Why?

_____

3. What qualities do you think the writer might have that are not mentioned?

_____

Spotlight: Writing

A Find and correct at least 13 errors in this cover letter.

89 parker St
Mashburn IL 40877

May 16, 2005

Linda hooper
Director
Excite marketing
445 Broad Ave
Evanston, Il

Dear Mx. Hooper:

I write inresponse to your ad for an administrative assistant in the *Evanston Herald* on May 11. I would will enjoy the opportunity to meet you to speak about this position.

As you can see in the enclosed résumé, I work as an office clerk for three years. I started when I was in high school. My father moved here from Michigan (he got a better job). I am very organized and I like to work with people. I have good computer skills. My mother says I have a nice phone voice, too. Even though I'm only twenty, I am a hard worker.

I am very interested in the position of administrative assistant at Excited Marketing. I would appreciate the opportunity to discus my qualifications in person.

Sincerely

Katie Grant

B Read the letter in Activity A. List three things in the letter that don't need to be included.

1. _____

2. _____

3. _____

C Rewrite the second paragraph of the letter in Activity A and include only the relevant information.

_____

_____

_____

_____

_____

D Look at the template below. On a separate piece of paper write a cover letter for a job.

Your name
Your address
Your phone number

Date

Recipient's Name
Recipient's Job
Recipient's Address

Dear _____:

Write about the job you want to apply for, how you heard about the job, and when you heard about the job.

Highlight important information on your résumé that shows you can do the job you are applying for.

Thank the recipient for their attention and say when you will contact them for an interview.

Sincerely,

Sign your name

Type your name

Are you talking to me?

A Look at the photos. Match the photos to the descriptions below.

A

B

C

D

E

F

1. _____ He is not telling the truth.
2. _____ He is expressing his approval.
3. _____ He is showing that he won.
4. _____ She is shrugging because she doesn't know.
5. _____ She is going to ask a question.
6. _____ He is asking for quiet.

B Write sentences about what you think each person is doing.

A. _She is shrugging because her teacher asked her where her homework was._

B. _____

C. _____

D. _____

E. _____

F. _____

C Answer the questions about yourself.

1. What are three ways that you communicate with your friends and family?

   _____

2. Who are the three people you talk to most?

   _____

3. What is one way you communicate today that you didn't use ten years ago?

   _____

4. What is one way you will communicate in ten years that you don't use now?

   _____

D Complete the conversations.

1. A: Nice to meet you.

   B: _____

2. A: Can you help me with this?

   B: _____

3. A: I am so sorry. I didn't see you.

   B: _____

4. A: Could you wait a minute?

   B: _____

5. A: I'm really tired.

   B: _____

6. A: Do you have a minute? I've got a problem.

   B: _____

2
LESSON

Can I give you a hand?

A Classify the following remarks.

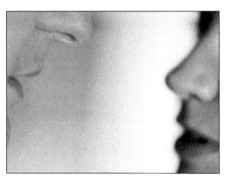

What is the person doing?

1. Excuse me. I hate to disturb you.   *Interrupting*

2. Is that clear?   _____

3. Could you pick up the supplies?   _____

4. Thanks so much. I was having trouble.   _____

5. I apologize. I wasn't paying attention.   _____

6. May I help?   _____

7. You should do this again. It's too messy.   _____

8. Good work.   _____

9. How do you like the new office?   _____

10. You could call ahead for reservations.   _____

B Circle the most appropriate (polite) response.

1. Why don't you put the box over there?

   A. No way.   B. Thanks for the suggestion, but . . .

2. Great job. That looks really nice.

   A. You're right.   B. Do you think so? Thanks.

3. I am so sorry. I didn't see you.

   A. That's okay. Don't worry.   B. Watch out next time.

4. Is there anything that isn't clear?

    A. Yes. The whole thing.   B. Sorry, could you go over it again?

5. Could you help Marie on the project?

    A. No, I don't like her.   B. I'd like to, but I'm really busy.

C Look at one of the responses you didn't choose in Activity B. Write the response and explain why it is not appropriate.

_____

_____

_____

D Read the emails below. What is the purpose for each email?

⊠ ⊟ ⊞	✉ doctor's appoint...		
Reply	Reply All	Print	Inbox

From: Lisa@undercover.net
Date: Thursday, May 5, 2005 3:05 PM
To: Annhood@undercover.net
Subject: doctor's appointment

Ann,

I have a doctor's appointment tomorrow afternoon.
Could you take my lunch shift? I'd be happy to
work your dinner shift.
Let me know.

Thanks,
Lisa

⊠ ⊟ ⊞	✉ presentation		
Reply	Reply All	Print	Inbox

From: Beth Nixon
Date: Tuesday, May 17, 2005 8:05 AM
To: Matt Carpenter
Subject: presentation

Matt,

Thanks again for your great work on the presentation
yesterday. I think it went very well. I'm sure we'll get
some new business from it.

Beth Nixon

Purpose: _____

Purpose: _____

E You were supposed to meet your daughter's teacher yesterday at 3:00. Unfortunately, you had to work late and you did not have the school's phone number with you. Write a note to the teacher expressing your regret.

_____

_____

_____

_____

_____

LESSON 3

Could I interrupt for a minute?

A Write the responses from the box to complete the conversation.

> I don't think so, but if I do, I'll ask. Thanks.
> Yes?
> Oh, I'm sorry. Can you tell me what's wrong with it?
> Sure. What is it?
> I guess I was so worried about getting it done on time, I wasn't very careful.

Supervisor: Could I interrupt you for a minute, Sam?

Sam: _____

Supervisor: I'd like to talk to you about this report.

Sam: _____

Supervisor: Well, the thing is, it's not done very well.

Sam: _____

Supervisor: I don't think the numbers in this chart are correct, and there are a lot of spelling and grammar mistakes.

Sam: _____

Supervisor: I understand. If you need more time or more help, you should ask for it. Do you need help rewriting this?

Sam: _____

B Answer the questions about the conversation in Activity A.

1. Who interrupts? _____

2. Who gives feedback? _____

3. Who asks for feedback? _____

4. Who expresses regret? _____

5. Who offers help? _____

6. Who expresses appreciation? _____

C Circle the correct form of the words in **bold**.

1. Be careful when you **interrupt/interruption**. Some **interrupts/interruptions** are impolite.

2. If my boss **criticizes/criticisms** me, I get a little upset.

3. If someone gives Vera a gift, she shows her **appreciate/appreciation** by sending a card.

4. Jon's boss makes lots of **suggests/suggestions**.

5. You should **express/expression** regret when you make a mistake.

6. A good teacher checks for **understand/understanding**.

7. People need to learn to **communicate/communication** better.

8. I'm really nervous. I have to **present/presentation** the new product at a meeting tomorrow.

★ ★

TAKE IT OUTSIDE: Interview a family member, friend, or coworker. Write their answers.

1. What communication problem(s) have you had recently at work, school, or home? _____

_____

2. What did you do about it? _____

_____

3. What could you do differently next time to handle the problem? _____

_____

★ ★

Being a Good Communicator

A Answer the questions using complete sentences.

1. What are some differences in communication between your culture and American culture? _____

   _____

2. Have you ever had a problem communicating because of a cultural difference? What was the problem and

   why do you think it happened? _____

   _____

B Read the article.

In today's global business world, the ability to communicate across different cultures is very important. Whether it's at work, at school, or in your community, chances are you will come into contact with people from another culture. Here are some tips to make your cross-cultural communication more succesful:

- Look for what you have in common with people from another culture rather than what separates you from them. No matter what culture another person comes from, you two are more similar than different.

- Share information about your culture and ask about theirs. Remember that your customs are probably a little different. When there is a communication problem, check to see if it is because of a cultural difference.

- Although the people from a culture may be similar in a lot of ways, they are not all the same. Remember you are communicating with one person, not with the entire group.

- When you have a disagreement with someone from another culture, offer any criticism in private. Public criticism can be very embarassing. Treat the other person as an equal, not as someone below you. Also, be patient. Resolving disagreements with anyone can be time-consuming.

C Read the inferences about the article in Activity B. Check *True* or *False*. Then write a piece of evidence from the reading that supports your answer.

1. Nowadays people have to communicate with different cultures.

   ☐ True   ☐ False

   Evidence: _____

   _____

2. In talking to someone from another culture, you should remember that there are communication differences.

   ☐ True   ☐ False

   Evidence: _____

   _____

3. People from the same culture always communicate the same way.

   ☐ True   ☐ False

   Evidence: _____

   _____

4. If you have a problem with someone from another culture, it's best to try to forget about it.

   ☐ True   ☐ False

   Evidence: _____

   _____

D Cross out the word that has a dissimilar meaning.

1. in common   differences   similarities
2. separate   add   include
3. represent   belong to   dislike
4. global   worldwide   local
5. in private   public   one-on-one

E Complete the chart with information from the article in Activity B.

When communicating with someone from another culture	
Do	**Don't**

5 LESSON

What would you do?

A Paraphrase the sentences below. Write the real situation.

1. If I had a car, I would drive every day.

   I don't have a car. I don't drive every day.

2. If we lived in France, we would speak French.

   _____

3. Sara would have class today if it were Tuesday.

   _____

4. If they worked harder, they would finish faster.

   _____

B Write the correct form of the verb.

1. If he _____ (break) your stereo, he would buy you a new one.

2. I would tell her if she _____ (be) wrong.

3. If Mary _____ (like) your haircut, she would compliment you on it.

4. You _____ (ask) more questions if you could speak English better.

5. If I _____ (hurt) your feelings, I would apologize.

6. If they were busy, we _____ (not interrupt) them.

7. She would ask if she _____ (need) help.

8. If I _____ (know) what to do, I would tell you.

C Rewrite the sentences as unreal conditionals.

1. He doesn't have a job. He doesn't have money to pay the bills.

   If he had a job, he would have money to pay the bills.

2. Our school doesn't have a bookstore. We can't buy books here.

   _____

3. That house needs a lot of work. They won't buy it.

_____

4. Cell phones are fairly inexpensive. Many people own them.

_____

D Look at the photos. Write a sentence about what you would do in each situation.

1

2

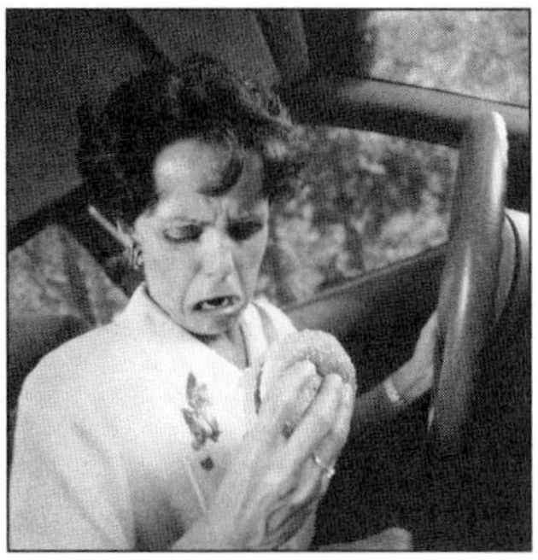

3

4

1. If I were the girl's parent, _____

2. If I witnessed a terrible accident, _____

3. _____

4. _____

E Write three sentences about what you would say if your teacher asked for some feedback on your class.

_____

_____

_____

I think that . . .

A Read the newspaper article and answer the questions using complete sentences.

Supervisor Parker Backs More Money For Schools.

Supervisor Diana Parker supports a proposal to provide $12 million more to city public schools over the next three years. She believes the money will allow schools to hire and retain better teachers and to expand art and music programs. Parker presented her proposal to the City Council Tuesday night.

The measure faces strong opposition from Supervisor Paul Grant. Grant believes the new school funds will mean big tax hikes for city residents.

The Board of Supervisors will vote on the proposal next month. On Monday, the board will hold an open forum for community members to voice their opinions.

1. Who wants to spend more money on schools?

   _____

2. Who is against spending more money on schools?

   _____

3. What is one reason the article mentions to spend more money on schools?

   _____

4. What is one reason against increased school spending?

   _____

5. How can community members help the Board of Supervisors decide what to do?

   _____

B Newspapers usually have a page on which they print letters to the editor. These letters are written by readers and usually express an opinion on an issue in the newspaper. Read the two letters to the editor below and complete the chart.

Parker Right To Support Schools

The writer is a sixth grader at Chesterbrook Middle School.

In response to "Council Member Parker Backs More Money For Schools" (Sept. 15):

Thank you, Diana Parker, for your support of schools. The money could be used to keep our good teachers. My teacher last year quit teaching because the pay was so low and the job was so difficult.

Our school doesn't have a music program anymore because we don't have the money, and we only have art once a week. I want to study music in college, but I won't be able to if I don't begin now.

Lydia Moore

Grant Has My Interests At Heart

Diana Parker, once again, wants to use taxpayers' hard-earned money to promote unnecessary programs in schools. Students need to spend more time on core subjects such as English and math. Music and art just take time away from the important subjects.

Paul Grant has my interests at heart when he opposes Parker's plan. He speaks for the taxpayer, the hard-working members of the community who would rather keep taxes low and spend public money only on essentials.

Don Lee

	Lydia Moore	Don Lee
Who does the writer agree with?		
What reasons does the writer give?		

★ ★

TAKE IT OUTSIDE: Read a letter to the editor in your local newspaper. Answer the questions.

1. What is the issue? _____

_____

2. What is the writer's opinion? _____

_____

3. What is your opinion? _____

_____

★ ★

She has her performance evaluation today.

A Read the information about performance evaluations below and answer the questions. Use complete sentences.

PERFOMANCE EVALUATIONS

1. Performance evaluations should take place once a year. Supervisors should evaluate employees after giving notice, and then conduct announced observations. Employees will also have the opportunity to provide upward evaluations, that is, to answer questionnaires about their supervisor's performance.

2. After observations, supervisors will complete the evaluation form (see appendix 1A), and then schedule a face-to-face interview with each employee. In the interview, the supervisor will give the employee a copy of the form and explain the evaluation. The employee may ask questions at that time or schedule another time to ask questions about the evaluation.

3. All evaluations (employee and upward) should follow certain guidelines. Comments should be specific and focus on facts not opinions. For example, "Janice did not turn her quarterly report in on 10/19 as requested," is more specific than "Janice is often disorganized and late with assignments." Comments should relate to workplace behaviors, not personality ("My supervisor is mean and difficult."). Comments should not be general or ambiguous ("Ron might want to work a little harder at some things").

4. If an employee still disagrees with the evaluation after discussion with the supervisor, he or she can submit an appeal in writing. The appeal should state the reasons for the disagreement and provide facts to support his or her position. Call the Human Resources Office for more information.

1. How often do supervisors evaluate employees? _____

2. What do supervisors have to do before an evaluation? _____

3. What do supervisors do after completing the evaluation form? _____

_____

4. What can employees do if they think the evaluation is wrong? _____

B Read the pairs of sentences. Circle the letter of the sentence that follows the guidelines given in Activity A. Then give a reason for your answer.

1. A. "Mr. Peters is lazy and messy."
   B. "Mr. Peters left his tools lying out in his workspace on 12/16."

   Reason: _____

   _____

2. A. "Hannah answers the phone politely and asks visitors to have a seat."
   B. "Hannah is funny and enjoyable to be around."

   Reason: _____

   _____

★ ★

TAKE IT OUTSIDE: Talk to a family member, friend, or supervisor and ask about three things that were covered in their most recent performance evaluation.

_____

_____

_____

★ ★

TAKE IT ONLINE: Use your favorite search engine and enter "employee evaluation." Write three things that you learn.

_____

_____

_____

Practice Test

REVIEW

LESSON

DIRECTIONS: Read the information about interviews to answer the next five questions. Use the Answer Sheet.

How to Handle a Job Interview

1. Answer questions completely. Sometimes the interviewer will ask a question that has more than one part. Make sure you address all parts of the question in your answer.

2. Look the interviewer in the eye. Eye contact suggests that you are honest and open. Looking away may indicate that you are unreliable.

3. Smile, but not too much. You want to appear friendly but sincere.

4. Most interviewers will expect to shake your hand. Be alert to this and give a firm handshake.

5. Come prepared with questions. Most interviewers will ask if you have any. Asking questions shows your interest.

1. Where should you look during the interview?
   A. You should look down at your résumé.
   B. You should keep your eyes moving.
   C. You should look in the interviewer's eyes.
   D. You should look generally at the interviewer.

2. In which part will you find information about answering questions?
   A. Part 1
   B. Part 5
   C. Part 2
   D. Part 3

3. Which part talks about shaking hands?
   A. Part 5
   B. Part 4
   C. Part 3
   D. Part 2

4. Which statement is true according to the information?
   A. You should smile a lot.
   B. You should smile but not a lot.
   C. You should look serious.
   D. You should frown.

5. Why should you ask questions?
   A. to show you are interested
   B. because you don't know anything
   C. to keep the interview going
   D. to show your English skills

ANSWER SHEET

	A	B	C	D
1	Ⓐ	Ⓑ	Ⓒ	Ⓓ
2	Ⓐ	Ⓑ	Ⓒ	Ⓓ
3	Ⓐ	Ⓑ	Ⓒ	Ⓓ
4	Ⓐ	Ⓑ	Ⓒ	Ⓓ
5	Ⓐ	Ⓑ	Ⓒ	Ⓓ
6	Ⓐ	Ⓑ	Ⓒ	Ⓓ
7	Ⓐ	Ⓑ	Ⓒ	Ⓓ
8	Ⓐ	Ⓑ	Ⓒ	Ⓓ
9	Ⓐ	Ⓑ	Ⓒ	Ⓓ
10	Ⓐ	Ⓑ	Ⓒ	Ⓓ

DIRECTIONS: Refer to the email below to answer the next five questions. Use the Answer Sheet on page 156.

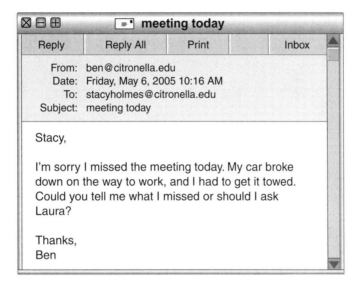

⊠ ⊟ ⊞   ✉ **meeting today**

| Reply | Reply All | Print | Inbox |

From: ben@citronella.edu
Date: Friday, May 6, 2005 10:16 AM
To: stacyholmes@citronella.edu
Subject: meeting today

Stacy,

I'm sorry I missed the meeting today. My car broke down on the way to work, and I had to get it towed. Could you tell me what I missed or should I ask Laura?

Thanks,
Ben

6. Who wrote the message?

A. Stacy

B. Ben

C. Citronella

D. Laura

7. What is the subject of the email?

A. meeting today

B. the car

C. a tow truck

D. work

8. What is the purpose of the email?

A. to criticize

B. to express appreciation

C. to check for understanding

D. to express regret

9. What does the writer NOT do?

A. express regret

B. make a request

C. ask for feedback

D. express appreciation

10. Who did Ben have a meeting with?

A. Laura

B. Stacy

C. Laura and Stacy

D. his supervisor

HOW DID YOU DO? Count the number of correct answers on your answer sheet. Record this number in the bar graph on the inside back cover.

Spotlight: Reading

A Reread the letters. Write down two facts and two opinions stated in the letters.

The Herald Forum

Parker Right to Support Schools
The writer is a sixth grader at Chesterbrook Middle School.
In response to "Council Member Parker backs more money for schools" (Sept. 15):

Thank you, Diana Parker, for your support of schools. The money could be used to keep our good teachers. My teacher last year quit teaching because the pay was so low and the job was so difficult.

Our school doesn't have a music program anymore because we don't have the money, and we only have art once a week. I want to study music in college, but I won't be able to if I don't begin now.
Lydia Moore

Grant Has My Interests At Heart

Diana Parker, once again, wants to use taxpayers' hard-earned money to promote unnecessary programs in schools. Students need to spend more time on core subjects such as English and math. Music and art just take time away from the important subjects.

Paul Grant has my interests at heart when he opposes Parker's plan. He speaks for the taxpayer, the hard-working members of the community who would rather keep taxes low and spend public money only on essentials.
Don Lee

Fact 1: _____

Fact 2: _____

Opinion 1: _____

Opinion 2: _____

B Read the paragraph and complete the chart.

On February 1, the board voted overwhelmingly to approve a 4% pay raise for all employees. As department head, I thought the board members' decision showed excellent judgment. Without the pay raises, I believe we would have trouble keeping the wonderful teaching staff we currently have. Starting July 15, all employees will receive the 4% raise. Employees who meet certain requirements, such as superior evaluations and at least 5 years employment) will receive an additional 1%. Any questions should be directed to Human Resources.

158

Facts	Opinions

C Read the statements below. Identify one fact and one opinion in each.

1. "In my country, Peru, men touch more often than American men do. I think it's very strange that men here don't touch."

   Fact: _____

   Opinion: _____

2. "Students in most Asian countries are used to the teacher giving lectures. It's a better way to learn."

   Fact: _____

   Opinion: _____

3. "Kissing people on the cheek is a strange way to greet people. It's more common in Europe than it is in the United States."

   Fact: _____

   Opinion: _____

4. "It's very disrespectful when people don't maintain eye contact. My coworker doesn't look me in the eye very often, and I don't trust her."

   Fact: _____

   Opinion: _____

Spotlight: Writing

A Read the following statements and write *Agree* or *Disagree* to express your opinion.

1. Parents should help their children with their schoolwork. _____

2. Community members need to volunteer their time. _____

3. It's more important to spend time with your family than to make money. _____

4. Workers should never talk back to their supervisors. _____

5. It's not a good idea to express your anger openly. _____

6. People communicate differently in the United States than they do in my country. _____

B Choose one of the statements from Activity A and brainstorm ideas that support your opinion. Use a cluster diagram to indicate reasons and then add details (see page 20).

C Create an outline from your cluster diagram in Activity B.

D Write a paragraph of at least ten sentences expressing your opinion.

Correlation Table

Student Book Pages	Workbook Pages
Pre-Unit	
2–3	
Unit 1	
4–5	2–3
6–7	4–5
8–9	6–7
10–11	8–9
12–13	10–11
14–15	12–15
16–17	16–17
18–19	18–19
20–21	20–21
Unit 2	
22–23	22–23
24–25	24–25
26–27	26–27
28–29	28–29
30–31	30–31
32–33	32–35
34–35	36–37
36-37	38–39
38-39	40–41

Student Book Pages	Workbook Pages
Unit 3	
40–41	42–43
42–43	44–45
44–45	46–47
46–47	48–49
48–49	50–51
50–51	52–55
52–53	56–57
54–55	58–59
56–57	60–61
Unit 4	
58–59	62–63
60–61	64–65
62–63	66–67
64–65	68–69
66–67	70–71
68–69	72–75
70–71	76–77
72–73	78–79
74-75	80–81

Student Book Pages	Workbook Pages		Student Book Pages	Workbook Pages
Unit 5			**Unit 7**	
76–77	82–83		112–113	122–123
78–79	84–85		114–115	124–125
80–81	86–87		116–117	126–127
82–83	88–89		118–119	128–129
84–85	90–91		120–121	130–131
86–87	92–95		122–123	132–135
88–89	96–97		124–125	136–137
90–91	98–99		126–127	138–139
92–93	100–101		128–129	140–141
Unit 6			**Unit 8**	
94–95	102–103		130–131	142–143
96–97	104–105		132–133	144–145
98–99	106–107		134–135	146–147
100–101	108–109		136–137	148–149
102–103	110–111		138–139	150–151
104–105	112–115		140–141	152–155
106–107	116–117		142–143	156–157
108–100	118–119		144–145	158-159
110–111	120–121		146–147	160–161

Photo Credits

From the Getty Images Royalty-Free Collection: p. 2; p. 4, right; p. 5, right; p. 11, left; p. 13; p. 14; p. 18; p. 22, left; p. 22, right; p. 24, left; p. 24, right; p. 27, top; p. 27, bottom; p. 31; p. 32, top; p. 32, middle; p. 32, bottom; p. 39, left; p. 43, left; p. 43, middle; p. 44; p. 46; p. 47, top; p. 47, bottom; p. 51; p. 52; p. 53; p. 54, mixer; p. 54, yoga class; p. 58; p. 60; p. 62, left; p. 62, right; p. 63, left; p. 70; p. 76; p. 78, middle; p. 78, bottom; p. 79; p. 80; p. 82, top middle; p. 82, top right; p. 82, bottom left; p. 82, bottom middle; p. 84, top left; p. 84, top middle; p. 84, top right; p. 84, bottom right; p. 89, top; p. 89, middle; p. 91; p. 99; p. 100, right; p. 104, skateboarding; p. 104, graffiti; p. 104, litter; p. 105, top left; p. 105, top right; p. 105, bottom left; p. 105, bottom right; p. 106; p. 108, top; p. 108, middle; p. 108, bottom; p. 111, left; p. 111, right; p. 112; p. 117; p. 118; p. 119, right; p. 123, top left; p. 123, middle left; p. 123, bottom left; p. 123, bottom right; p. 124, left; p. 124, right; p. 125; p. 128; p. 130; p. 135; p. 138; p. 142, top middle; p. 142, bottom left; p. 142, bottom middle; p. 144; p. 146; p. 151, top right; p. 154; p. 155; p. 159, photo 2; p. 159, photo 4;

From the CORBIS Royalty-Free Collection: p. 4, left; p. 5, left; p. 11, right; p. 25, left; p. 25, right; p. 26; p. 30; p. 39, right; p. 43, right; p. 54, weight training; p. 63, right; p. 64; p. 69, top; p. 69, bottom; p. 78, top; p. 82, bottom right; p. 86; p. 87; p. 89, bottom; p. 92; p. 100, left; p. 104, dogs; p. 104, bottle; p. 123, top right; p. 126; p. 133; p. 142, top left; p. 142, top right; p. 142, bottom right; p. 148; p. 151, top left; p. 151, bottom left; p. 151, bottom right; p. 159, photo 3;

Other Images: p. 6: Bob Daemmrich/The Image Works; p. 66: Bob Daemmrich/The Image Works; p. 82, top left: Dennis Wise/Getty Images; p. 84, bottom left: James Leynse/CORBIS; p. 119, left: Emily A. White; p. 123, middle right: Bob Daemmrich/The Image Works; p. 152: Alistair Berg/Getty Images; p. 159, photo 1: Sean Cayton/The Image Works.